PEAU DE CHAGRIN

PEAU DE CHAGRIN

or,

The Skin of Pain

A PLAY IN FIVE ACTS AND SEVEN SCENES

by

LOUIS JUDICIS

Translated and Adapted by FRANK J. MORLOCK

THE BORGO PRESS

An Imprint of Wildside Press LLC

MMIX

www.wildsidepress.com

FIRST EDITION

CONTENTS

Cast of Characters 7

Prologue, Scene I.. 9
Act I, Scene II... 31
Act II, Scene III 44
Act III, Scene IV 58
Act IV, Scene V.. 91
Act V, Scene VI... 110
Epilogue, Scene VII 134

About the Author... 138
About the Translator.. 139

DEDICATION

This play is dedicated to *Jackie Stanton*,
sometimes known as Dagny, for
all the help she has given me
over the years in preparing
my plays for publication.

With sincere thanks.

PEAU DE CHAGRIN, BY LOUIS JUDICIS

CAST OF CHARACTERS

RAPHAEL
RASTIGNAC
JOB
HAMILCAR
DE RANCY
JOB'S SALESMAN
PAPA JACQUES
GUILLAUME
A NOTARY
A SERVANT
A WAITER IN A RESTAURANT
FOEDORA
PAULINE
SIMONNE
MADAME GAUDIN
EUPHRASIE
MADAME GERVAIS
GERTRAU DE SWIEBELAUGEN

PEAU DE CHAGRIN, BY LOUIS JUDICIS

PROLOGUE

SCENE I

The Woman Without a Heart

A garret. Elegant, but old, worn furniture. A piano in a corner.

PAULINE: (entering, carrying linen which she places in a drawer in the chest of drawers) If he knew that I stayed up all night to darn and mend his wardrobe, he'd get up-set. But Bah! A scientist, always distracted. He never notices a thing. It's a pleasure to serve him. And then, don't I owe him gratitude? Didn't he teach me music, design, grammar—in the end all that I know? Thanks to him, I will soon be in a condition to give lessons in my turn. Then we will have a servant and my poor mother will no longer be alone taking care of this hotel, when

9

she's dying of fatigue. (looking out the window) How the rain is falling! The sky is set for the whole day. Where can he be in such weather? Ah, at the home of that woman, doubtless, at the home of the Countess that his friend Mr. Rastignac introduced him to. A coquette, a great rich lady and proud, who will, after having driven him crazy, cause him to die of despair! Oh! That woman! I hate her! She's really lucky, she is! (drying a tear) What am I thinking about? My God this rain worries me. He's going to come back soaked to the bone, trembling with fever for he's too economical to take a carriage. (smiling sadly) Economical! Poor boy, and no fire in the month of December. (cupping her ear) I hear a noise.—It's him. (examining him) O my God! How pale he is. (Raphael enters without seeing Pauline; coat buttoned, collar turned up. He is agitated and shakes his hat, which streams.)

RAPHAEL: Oh! Misery! misery! Had to spend thirty sous to take a cab, and here are my last clothes ruined.

PAULINE: (timidly) Hello, Mr. Raphael.

RAPHAEL: (aside) Oh! To see her again, one time—a single time. (examining his hat) With this hat? Curse! (hurling himself with rage on his bed) Oh, Money! Money! (opens and shuts the drawers of his chest of drawers rapidly) Nothing! Nothing! (noticing Pauline) Pauline! did you come to take your lesson, child?

PAULINE: I don't have the courage to work when I see you so unhappy.

RAPHAEL: (taking her excitedly by the hand) Unhappy! Oh, yes! Pauline! why am I not rich?

PAULINE: Your hand is burning. You have a fever, Mr. Raphael. That woman will kill you.

RAPHAEL: (pulling his hand away) To excite the pity of that child! (aloud) You're right, Pauline. I don't feel well, I'm ill.

PAULINE: And then, you don't take care of yourself anymore. You haven't eaten today.

RAPHAEL: (aside, feeling his pockets with a bitter smile) That's true.

PAULINE: We had some good cream this morning. I'm going to find you some.

RAPHAEL: No Pauline, I won't permit—

MADAME GAUDIN: (entering with a warm bowl of cream in her hand) We'll see about that.

PAULINE: Good mother!

RAPHAEL: Excellent woman.

MADAME GAUDIN: (giving him, a cup) Come on, drink. That will refresh you.

RAPHAEL: (after drinking) I needed it.

MADAME GAUDIN: It's really fortunate that it suits him. My God, how clammy he is. Do you want to kill yourself with cold?

RAPHAEL: (aside) Kill myself! Oh! yes—death rather than this frightful torture. (sadly to Pauline) You remember, Pauline, that passage where Bossuet describes God to us, rewarding a glass of water more richly than a victory?

PAULINE: Yes.

RAPHAEL: (taking her hand) Well, as it's possible we will leave each other soon, let me prove my gratitude for the cares that you and your mother have had for me.

12

PAULINE: Leave us! You want to leave us?

RAPHAEL: My piano is one of the best instruments of Erard. Accept it. (Pauline gestures negatively) Take it without scruples. I really don't know how to take it on the trip I expect to make.

PAULINE: (aside) O! My God—he frightens me.

MADAME GAUDIN: A trip! And where do you intend to go, if you please? (looking around her) Damn! This isn't a luxury hotel, the Saint Quentin, it's true—but since you haven't died, in three years, you must have acclimatized yourself to it by now.

RAPHAEL: With the profits from the sale of my furniture, Madame Gaudin, you will pay yourself all that I owe you.

MADAME GAUDIN: Ah! I understand. You are blushing to be a little in arrears with us. The gentleman is proud because he's a Marquis.

RAPHAEL: (surprised) Who told you?

MADAME GAUDIN: Don't I know all your story? Go

on, go on. Old Jonathan, the former servant of your late father, who came from time to time to ask news of you. Old Jonathan's informed me of fine things on your account.

RAPHAEL: What do you mean?

MADAME GAUDIN: (taking his head in her hands) Poor cherub—so big! as noble as handsome! Yes, yes—the dear man told me everything. I know you sold your mother's inheritance—600,000 francs to pay the debts of the late Marquis, your father, who ruined himself in business affairs. That done, you still had 15,000 francs with which to live for three years. Ah, damn! Not enough to keep a carriage. But still, it was your business to use judgment and economy. (counting on her fingers) Sixty francs for rent, three sous for bread per day, two sous for milk, three sous for the butcher.

RAPHAEL: Mercy, enough.

MADAME GAUDIN: After that, if you had strength to make a few debts—it's nothing to blush for—. Does Mama Gaudin demand something of you? I am proud, too, Mr. Raphael, and have a right to be. If you are a Marquis, I am a Baroness, Baroness de Witschnaur, by the grace of the Emperor who understood how to make nobles! This little one you see is the god-child of Princess Borghese. With all deference to yourself, and if my poor Gaudin hadn't let himself be captured by the Russians at Beresina, my Pauline would have been raised to the Legion of Honor just like a crowd of Duchesses and Princesses.

PAULINE: They would have made me leave my good mother. And then, what would I have learned more than here?

MADAME GAUDIN: As to that, it's true. You are as smart as an Empress. And it counts for nothing to him and he pretends he owes me money—and he wants to leave us so as not to increase his debt.

RAPHAEL: My good Madame Gaudin, it's necessary.

MADAME GAUDIN: No! It's not necessary. I tell you, you will stay in the Hotel Saint Quentin and so long as there's a slice of bread in the buffet, you will have your share. Besides, I've the idea we will become rich one day. You will perhaps really find a library for your great work, and we—You know that Miss Lenormand sustains doggedly that Gaudin didn't die in Siberia, but that he found a way to escape and go make his fortune in the Indies. He'll return someday, be sure of it. Tonight, I read John The Evangelist, while Pauline held suspended from her fingers a key attached to a Bible. And the key turned! It's a sign that Gaudin is well and prosperous. I saw him in a dream, in a vessel full of serpents, but happily the water was troubled; that signifies gold or precious stones from overseas. But, I'm amusing myself gossiping, and meanwhile my charcoal is burning. (retaking the cup she brought) Come; goodbye, ingrate. And good courage!

PAULINE: (holding out her hand to Raphael) Goodbye, Mr. Raphael.

RAPHAEL: Goodbye, Pauline. (the women leave, Raphael watches Pauline as she goes) Charming child! What simplicity, what grace, what heart! Oh—why don't I love her! What has God placed this fatal love in my heart for? Which I cannot triumph over and which is killing me! Fool, who had before his eyes the example of every devotion and allows himself to fall for the grimaces of calculated egoism! Oh, yes, quite foolish, for me who, once smitten, like Pygmalion with a marble statue burned my heart at the feet of an icy idol. And for a long while I accepted this coldness in exchange for my flame, this scorn in exchange for my adoration! No; no; enough humiliation, enough cowardice. The hour has come when I must be a man. (looking sadly at papers spread on the table) Oh, my unfinished work, oh, my writings, cherished fruit of my vigils, you, that so long consoled me in my misery! You, who would have given me glory, fortune, perhaps. I must say goodbye to you. Goodbye, forever. (turns, hearing Rastignac enter) Rastignac!

RASTIGNAC: (entering) Myself, my dear fellow, coming to ask a service of you.

RAPHAEL: (excitedly) A service! Speak, my friend.

RASTIGNAC: Loan me ten crowns.

RAPHAEL: (laughing with effort) Ten crowns! Ah, by Jove, you've come to the right place.

RASTIGNAC: You don't have them, perhaps?

RAPHAEL: Perhaps. Now, there's a pretty word.

RASTIGNAC: Never mind—give me what you can. Fifty francs, twenty francs, one hundred sous. One hundred sous. Everybody has one hundred sous—What the Devil, except me.

RAPHAEL: And me! My dear fellow. Such as you see

me, on an empty stomach since yesterday, but for the charity of my hostess.

RASTIGNAC: The Devil! Now there's something which furiously overturns the edifice of my fortune. And such a pretty system!

RAPHAEL: What—it was for gambling?

RASTIGNAC: What do you want? Yesterday evening I lost right down to my last sou—and under the penalty of missing out on a golden opportunity, I must have a thousand shillings in an hour—a gift, a bribe that I promised to the mistress of a capitalist.

RAPHAEL: A business affair, a bribe! Then you've given up medicine?

RASTIGNAC: Eh! It's given me up. The sick have become a myth, a poetic fantasy, a thing of mist and impalpable.—Then you don't have a sou? Let's not talk about it any more. At least you're lucky in love. And the beautiful Foedora?

RAPHAEL: Foedora! My friend, that woman is killing me. I prefer death to the existence she's giving me. And I am trying conscientiously to find the best way of ending the struggle. What do you think of opium?

RASTIGNAC: Bah! Atrocious suffering.

RAPHAEL: Asphyxiation?

RASTIGNAC: Coarse!

RAPHAEL: The Seine?

RASTIGNAC: Yuck! The Morgue.

RAPHAEL: A pistol shot?

RASTIGNAC: And if you miss? A jaw ripped off; a charming invention to please the ladies.

RAPHAEL: There must still be a way to end it.

RASTIGNAC: Doubtless—Marry her.

RAPHAEL: You are stupid.

RASTIGNAC: My word, no. I will end that way myself. My pretty widow doesn't want to listen to anything except marriage. A charming person. I will make you see her. An Alsatian, a bit chubby! She reads Kant, Schiller,

Jean Paul and a crowd of books on hydraulics; she weeps downpours reading Goethe. Twenty-five thousand pounds income, my dear boy, and the tiniest foot, the prettiest hand on earth. Ah, if she didn't have an accent, she would be an accomplished woman.

RAPHAEL: You can laugh. You are lucky.

RASTIGNAC: First of all, my good friend, remember that philosophic maxim. There are no unhappy people— except for those who wish to be. Now, where are you at with the beautiful Muscovite?

RAPHAEL: A bit further from the goal than I was three months ago, when, through my ill luck, you took me to her home. That day, she gave herself to coquetry; she was likeable, caressing, almost affectionate.

RASTIGNAC: Doubtless—a scientist with blond hair, a Benedictine in yellow gloves. That was original.

RAPHAEL: I left ravished, seduced by the woman, intoxicated by the luxury, tickled by everything in my head that was noble, vicious, good, bad. Then, feeling myself so alive, so exalted, I thought I understood the attraction that led all those artists, those diplomats, those double stock jobbers, doubly corrugated like their strong boxes—to Foedora. Without doubt they came to find near her the delirious emotion which vibrates in me with all the strength of my being, whipping my blood in the smallest arteries and pounding in my skull! She gave herself to none, in order to keep all. A woman coquettish to that degree is such that she loves no one.

RASTIGNAC: Yes, but you often obtain from hate what you hope to obtain from love.

RAPHAEL: What do you mean?

RASTIGNAC: What do I know? a recollection, an involuntary allusion to certain rumors spread about Foedora.

RAPHAEL: Explain yourself!

RASTIGNAC: Foedora is vindictive, despotic; carried away in her hates. Do you know an enemy of hers she hates passionately to death? Well, make yourself her knight, her bravo, her bully. You will be her lover.

RAPHAEL: What! you, a man of intelligence, an observer, you echo these wretched slanders —!

RASTIGNAC: Slanders as much as you like. Still, your beautiful Countess left Moscow with a reputation equivocal enough. The Russian Ambassador fell to laughing when I spoke to him about her. He doesn't receive her and he greets her very casually if he meets her in the park.

RAPHAEL: Still, she sees everyone. Didn't she spend last season at the Château of the Maréchal de Ratisbonne?

RASTIGNAC: Oh, in France her reputation is intact. And then, she's a clever woman. She will recover like the most agile diplomat. In short, you fell badly in love.

RAPHAEL: I came back on foot from the Faubourg Saint Honoré where Foedora lives. Between her hotel and the rue de la Harpe, there's almost all of Paris; but the way seemed short to me, and yet it was cold. To undertake the conquest of Foedora in winter, a rough winter, when I haven't thirty francs in my possession, when the distance between us was so great! Bah! Foedora or death, I shouted to myself, going around a bridge, Foedora is happiness. When I arrived here in my garret, naked and cold, I was still surrounded by Foedora's prodigious luxury. That contrast was a bad counselor. Here, shaking with rage, I cursed my decency and honest misery, my fecund garret where so many thoughts germinated. I demanded a reckoning from God, my father, the whole universe, and I put myself to bed completely famished, grumbling laughable imprecations, but totally deter-mined to seduce Foedora.

RASTIGNAC: And the next day you returned to see her!

RAPHAEL: The next day, the day after, everyday. Who wouldn't think himself loved in my situation? She en-couraged my attentions. If, sometimes I arrived much later than midnight there were charming sulks, adorable pouts, which made me fall at her feet. I was her cavalier servante. I accompanied her everywhere, walking, at the Opera, and, God forgive me, to church. Ah, how many unknown sacrifices I made for this woman. Let my work go—and fasting, that was nothing! But to cross the streets of Paris without letting myself get mud splat-tered, running to avoid the rain, arriving at her place as elegant as the fools she surrounds herself with. Ah—for an amorous and distracted poet—that task was full of difficulties and perils. My happiness, my love depended on a spot of mud on my only white coat! Not having five sous to pay a boot-black to clean it—a light imprint of dirt on my boots!

RASTIGNAC: In love, and covered with mud: a torture forgotten by Dante.

RAPHAEL: Well, this torture that seems so ridiculous to you—I endured with rage—and happiness. All the torments that I suffered, I suffered with delight. My flesh, my blood, my life, yes, I would give my life to the one who would tell me: Hope! Foedora will love you. Ah, it's necessary that this woman belong to me or that an abyss separate us. This morning I had a letter delivered to her in which I asked her for a supreme and final interview. Tonight, for the last time, perhaps, I will cross the door of her hotel.

FOEDORA: (entering) Don't take the trouble, Mr. Raphael.

RAPHAEL: (stupefied) Foedora! You here, Madame, at my place?

FOEDORA: Don't count on my liking it too much. I was bored. I went out in my carriage, and then, as I went by the Luxembourg, you know they must be having an interesting season there, it took my fancy to come ask for your arm.

RASTIGNAC: Oh, the implacable curiosity of women.

RAPHAEL: But how did you know where?

FOEDORA:—Your address that you hid with such obstinate discretion? Oh, by chance, only, I swear to you. This morning, one of your friends, Mr. de Rancy, left me your card with my chambermaid—instead of his own. (looking around her) You aren't well lodged, you know?

RAPHAEL: Madame, until this day, I've suffered from my poverty. I've not yet blushed for it. I must seem very guilty to you—for not being run off by your lackeys.

FOEDORA: Yes, you lied: you deceived me.

RAPHAEL: You don't look upon poverty as a crime?

FOEDORA: My dear sir, there are two sorts of poverty. One which goes boldly down the street in tatters, that relives Diogenes' life without realizing it, nourishing itself little, reducing life to simplicity, happier more than the rich, perhaps. Then there's another kind of poverty, an odious sort of poverty, the poverty of luxury, poverty in a white vest and yellow gloves. Spanish poverty, which conceals beggary behind a title. (meaningfully) Aren't you a Marquis?

RAPHAEL: Madame!

RASTIGNAC: That's brutal, but plain.

FOEDORA: Of the two types of poverty, you've chosen the worst, the least honorable. It's not my fault.

RAPHAEL: Well, so be it! Why should I hide it? Yes, to please you, I simulated riches and luxury. Would you have deigned to give me the alms of a single look if you had known that my pallor, about which you sometimes joked, Just Heaven—came from suffering, from hunger, for I was hungry at your feet, Countess! Is there a single one of your whims that didn't devour my entire fortune? Yesterday, even to offer you a bouquet, I sold—forgive me, God—my mother's portrait.

RASTIGNAC: Poor madman, who thinks to touch the heart of this woman by these means!

RAPHAEL: No, it's not possible, that God, who made you so beautiful, made you so—insensitive! My poverty—eh—what does my poverty matter? I know how much this burden weighs. Yet, I can still bear it—but, have a little pity on my love!

FOEDORA: Mr. Raphael—love is an investment, like any other. So much the worse for ninnies who let themselves be cheated with these prudent infatuations. Since my arrival in France, my fortune has been attempted by several young men. I have received declarations of love which would have been able to satisfy my pride. You cannot think it bad that I put my fortune and my person at a higher price than a madrigal! (Raphael gestures) Be sure, that I often sincerely reproach myself for your extravagant prodigalities. I ought to have found the perfume in the bouquets that cost you your dinner. I'm really ashamed of my ruinous fantasies, as you call them, now that I know the sum of your few shillings.

RASTIGNAC: (aside) A dismissal in perfect form!

RAPHAEL: (walking about agitatedly) Woman with no heart! woman with no heart! Oh, now, I know how it's possible to kill a woman!

RASTIGNAC: (coldly) And me, too.

FOEDORA: (terrified) Sir!

RAPHAEL: Foedora! Oh, pardon, pardon! I am mad. Me—threaten you! to attempt your life? I, who would give you all the hours that remain for me to live?

FOEDORA: All men, more or less, employ this classic

phrase. Allow me to withdraw.

RAPHAEL: (placing himself before her) Foedora—do you want to marry a millionaire?

FOEDORA: Perhaps, if he were a Duke. Goodbye, Marquis. (she leaves)

RASTIGNAC: Well, that's finished! Now, you're satisfied. You wanted an abyss between you two. Now there is one. Large enough and deep enough, I hope.

RAPHAEL: An abyss. Yes, it's there, engulfing me. Who will explain this terrible phenomenon of love? This woman railed at me, insulted me, outraged me with both hands. Well, rail at me, outrage me, in your turn, my friend. I will give ten years of my life to see her once again. To throw myself at her feet. To ask her pardon for all the wrong she's done me.

RASTIGNAC: And here I am, looking for a patient. Well, here's one, and, I hope one of the strongest sort.

RAPHAEL: That woman, I scorn her. Oh, to see her again for an hour. But hiding from her, in my turn, my luxury, a fabulous luxury, an Indian luxury, dazzling with the luster of my treasures. Oh! to be rich, my God!

to be rich.

RASTIGNAC: Decidedly—you're ill. You're staggering. Quickly take off those damp clothes for me.

RAPHAEL: Nothing, nothing—it's nothing. Oh—my head! my head!

RASTIGNAC: Put yourself in your bed. You must. I insist. I order you, as friend, as doctor.

RAPHAEL: (getting away) To avenge myself on Foedora. At that thought, you see, a shiver runs through my entire being. My eyes cloud up, the blood rushes through my head, and I choke. That's happiness!

RASTIGNAC: No, it's fever, a good and beautiful fever, perfectly developed.

RAPHAEL: You think so? Indeed, I feel very weak. I—I—(he falls)

RASTIGNAC: The Devil—Devil—brain fever. Congestion is to be feared. There's no time to lose. (he rings)

PAULINE: (entering) You rang, Mr. Raphael? (noticing him) Ah! My God—what's the matter with him? Raphael!

RASTIGNAC: Silence! and pray to God for him, Pauline. I'm going to try to save him.

(Pauline kneels near the bed. Rastignac leans over Raphael.)

CURTAIN

ACT I

SCENE II

An antique shop furnished with old furniture, Gothic trophies, bronzes, statues, pictures, arms and savage ornaments, skeletons and stuffed animals, etc. etc. It is almost dark.

At rise, a young man is sleeping in a curule chair. Raphael enters furtively.

RAPHAEL: An antique shop—perfect to kill time until evening. How many idlers on the quay. Impossible to drown peacefully. There are so many people ready to save you despite yourself! Humanity and then twenty-five francs for the police. To be fished out alive—that would be too ridiculous. And that Rastignac with his system. Gamblers all resemble each other. To hear them, it takes only one hand to amass millions. And they end by hanging themselves with their tie. For lack of a sou to purchase a rope. (the clerk wakes up and yawns noisily) Ah, there's someone here?

CLERK: (starting up) A customer. Heavens! I was going to close the shop.

RAPHAEL: Already!

CLERK: Oh, my boss, Mr. Job, wants it shut up at nightfall. Oil costs so much.

RAPHAEL: (aside) The Devil—

CLERK: Still, if the gentleman would like to see some objects of art, it's still light enough. We have antiques and curiosities of all sorts. (pointing to different objects) A crocodile from the Nile. Madame du Barry in the costume of a water nymph, the casket of Sesostris. The raft of Medusa in ivory, the bust of Papavoine in chocolate, the candy box of the Queen of Navarre.

RAPHAEL: (distracted, absently) A nice assortment, indeed.

CLERK: Here's the scissors of Jean Goujon. It bears the

imprint of the shot that killed the great artist on Saint Bartholomew's Day.

RAPHAEL: Authentic?

CLERK: Guaranteed, sir! A silk stocking coming from the wardrobe of the Man in the Iron Mask. An imitation in crystal of the diamond of the Great Mogul. An Englishman offered twenty-five crowns for it.

RAPHAEL: And you didn't give it to him?

CLERK: He wanted the original with it.

RAPHAEL: (aside, looking down the street) The strollers are becoming fewer. They're beginning to light the street lamps.

CLERK: A box of assignats found in the pocket of the Arab who assassinated General Kleber. Proof that England was subsidizing the enemies of France. (turning and seeing that Raphael is looking down the street) Goodness! You're not listening to me, sir?

RAPHAEL: Yes, yes—continue. It's very interesting.

CLERK: Perhaps, you're expecting someone?

RAPHAEL: (moving away from the window) Exactly, yes. I'm waiting for someone. A naturalist who intends to make some purchases here. (aside) We'll gain some time!

CLERK: That works out well. Yesterday we just received a complete collection of chaffinches of several species. So, if you would care to examine—

RAPHAEL: No need. (looking at a plaster box hung against the wall) What's that?

CLERK: A marvelous painting, they say. I've never seen it. Mr. Job has the key. If you wish, I will assume the risk of informing him.

RAPHAEL: You'll assume the risk? Is your Mr. Job some sort of Prince?

CLERK: Why, I don't know.

RAPHAEL: (looking through the window) That young man and that young girl won't leave! What can they be saying to each other for such a long while? Lovers, without doubt? Oh—love, a honeyed cup for some, poison for others! Why am I not that young man? Why isn't that young girl Foedora? Foedora? Ah, I don't want to think of that woman! (looking through the window) Gone! They're gone. At last. (Turns to go and finds himself nose to nose with Job who's been watching him for some minutes, an iron lamp in his hands. Job is an old man, dried out and thin. His coat is black velour, belted at the waist with a large silk cord. A black velour cap, a la Michel Angelo, laid flat on the skull, and allowing long strands of white hair to fall on each side of his face.)

RAPHAEL: (aside, frightened) Who is this spectre?

JOB: (examining him still, with suspicion; heavy Jewish accent) The gentleman wishes to see the portrait of Alexander the Great by Apelles?

RAPHAEL: (aside) Fool that I am! (aloud) You say?

JOB: The gentleman knows that Alexander found only Apelles worthy of putting him in a painting?

RAPHAEL: Yes, yes, I've read Quintus Curtius.

(Falls back to his reflections, while Job, after having placed his lamp in the shaft of a column, opens the box which contains the portrait.)

JOB: (disclosing the portrait) I covered the frame with gold sequins from head to toe.

RAPHAEL: (following his own train of thought) Still—got to die!

JOB: (grasping a stylus placed on a piece of furniture and putting himself in a defensive posture) You intend to murder me, Teufel!

RAPHAEL: Ah, sir, don't be afraid; it's a matter of my life, not yours.

JOB: (suspiciously) Ah, that's different!

RAPHAEL: While waiting for nightfall, to be able to drown myself without scandal, I came to see your riches. Who would not pardon this last pleasure to a man of science and poesy?

JOB: (replacing the stylus at his disposal) Have you been in a seminary for the last three years without a wife? Did your father reproach you too much for being born? Or have you been dishonored?

RAPHAEL: If I wanted to dishonor myself, I would keep

on living.

JOB: Don't you rather have the malady of gold—or the spleen? The spleen, that's very fashionable.

RAPHAEL: So as to relieve myself of revealing to you unheard of sufferings, which it is difficult to speak of in human language, I would tell you that I am in the most ignoble, the most acute of all poverty. (Job recoils rapidly, seizing his stylus anew) Reassure yourself, old man. I don't wish to beg either help or comfort.

JOB: (with a diabolical laugh) Eh! eh! Without that, I can console you—without giving you a French centime, a Spanish maravetis, a Venetian gazetta, an English farthing.

RAPHAEL: I know. The names of all the European currencies.

JOB: Without giving you anything in gold, silver, copper, paper, bonds, assignments or stocks, I can make you richer, more powerful, more eminent than a constitutional monarch.

RAPHAEL: (aside) What sort of madman am I dealing with?

JOB: (taking his lamp and directing the light toward an object affixed to the wall) Look at this little Peau de Chagrin.

RAPHAEL: (turning, after having looked at it for a moment) Well?

JOB: (taking it from the wall and placing it in Raphael's hands) Look at it. (lighting it with his lamp)

RAPHAEL: Ah! ah! here's the impression of the seal Orientals call the Mark of Solomon.

JOB: The gentleman knows it?

RAPHAEL: The sign, they say, has a fabulous power. (returning the talisman to him) Bah! Is there a man in the world simple enough to believe in the existence of this chimera?

JOB: (turning the talisman over) Since the gentleman is an orientalist, perhaps he will read this little sentence?

RAPHAEL: (taking it) It's from Sanskrit. (reading) "If you possess me, you will possesses everything. But your life belongs to me. Wish and your wish will be accomplished. But measure your wishes against your life. I will decrease your life span. Do you want me? Take me."

JOB: (aside) He's no longer thinking of dying.

RAPHAEL: (examining the talisman with great attention) And this line in imperceptible characters—which terminates the sentence? I cannot decipher it.

JOB: That's Chaldean.

RAPHAEL: Ah, I don't know that tongue.

JOB: (with a sardonic smile) Me, either.

RAPHAEL: (looking at him suspiciously) You lie!

JOB: (pretending indignation) Teufel! Give me back that talisman.

RAPHAEL: In a minute. (reading) "If you possess me, you will possess everything. Wish and your wish will be accomplished." (speaking) Yes, why, that's the thing. (reading) "At each wish I will decrease your life." (speaking) Isn't there some joke behind all this?

JOB: I offered this magic skin to men who said they feared neither God nor Devil. Well! None of them dared to touch it with the tip of his finger.

RAPHAEL: Why, you, yourself—you haven't tried?

JOB: Try! Mein Gott! If you were on top of the column in the Place de Vendome, would you try to hurl yourself to the pavement? Why would I have tempted the Devil? I don't want anything.

RAPHAEL: Nothing?

JOB: I know two terrible words, Mein Herr, two words which cause more trouble than all the cannons, all the bombs, all the engines of war. Those words are Will and Power.

RAPHAEL: (prodding the *peau de chagrin*) Will and Power. Why those are the two attributes of God.

JOB: Nein! Of the Devil. Will and power destroy us. The attribute of God is knowledge. To know is to be calm, tranquil, happy. The fool lives through his heart, through his senses. He dies young. Stupid. The wise man lives through his brain. Look at me, Mein Herr. I've known neither catarrh, nor cancer, nor paralysis, and I'm 102 years old.

RAPHAEL: A fine age!

JOB: (placing a finger on his face) To know is to be here—keep it. (pointing to the peau de chagrin) Will and Power. It's yours, I give it to you. This talisman is life. Life with its luxury, its splendors, its sensual pleasures. But it is a fast life, rapid, like flashing thunder. But it kills!

RAPHAEL: And what's your frigid science to me? What do I care about a languid, colorless life, proceeding sadly on its way to the tomb, without desires, without fears, without hope, without any of the tremblings of passion which shake our heart, boil our blood, and which scream to me that I am a man? A prompt life, rapid like lightning. Eh! Wasn't I going to give myself death, a vulgar death, an ignoble death! Suicide for suicide—I mean to be happy, a year, a month, a day, an hour! before casting my remains into the earth.

JOB: Fool!

RAPHAEL: Fool! yes—for all this is a trick, an Arab tale.

JOB: A trick—an Arab tale. Do you dare pronounce the cabalistic formula? You know it, I think.

RAPHAEL: (pressing the skin to his breast) Do you hope to make me go pale? Listen then: Mine your power! Mine your life! Master both! Slaves both! (hardly has he uttered these words when a flash of lightning, followed by a violent clap of thunder illuminates the stage)

JOB: (falling on his knees) Mein Gott! I am dead!

RAPHAEL: (stupefied momentarily) Eh, what! Satan obeys! The power of this talisman is real, then? On my soul, if it still belongs to me, I won't flinch! I want to enjoy all the sensual pleasures of life. I order this sinister power to dissolve all joys into one joy. I want to forget—in intoxication, in songs to wake the dead, songs whose sound will sweep over Paris like the crackling of a conflagration and rejuvenate even old geezers.

JOB: (rising) Young man, in the name of God, calm down. What you are wishing for is not pleasure, it's an orgy.

RAPHAEL: An orgy? So be it! And you will share it with me, nasty old geezer!

JOB: Me!

RAPHAEL: (as he leaves) To begin with, Job the Jew, Job the Usurer, Job the Centenarian, I want you to be drunken today and to fall in love with a chorus girl.

JOB: A chorus girl. My God, I am ruined. (running after Raphael) Have pity on me, young man, have pity on me!

(He rushes out, distracted.)

CURTAIN

ACT II

SCENE III

A Title Worth Six Millions

A vast hall or gallery, brilliantly lit. In the middle is a splendidly furnished table surrounded by young men, laughing, drinking, chatting. All the characters, except Raphael and Job who have yet to enter, sing the chorus after each of Rastignac's couplets.

CHORUS: (singing)
Children of folly
Let's brave the blows of fate
I ask you
What's needed to embellish life?
Drink to the lees,

PEAU DE CHAGRIN, BY LOUIS JUDICIS

Love to death.

RASTIGNAC:
While a vulgar miser
Gloats over his treasure,
Richer in my poverty,
I discern
At the bottom of my cup,
In the fiery medium
The shining fires of gold.

CHORUS: Children of folly, etc.

RASTIGNAC:
Of love that's purchased,
I'm not jealous.
A sweet little thing
Visits my room for nothing.
And with a discreet hand,
Slips the bolt into the lock.

CHORUS: Children of folly, etc.

RASTIGNAC:
Fie on politics
And intriguers, too.
Friends, my polemic

Far from philosophic
Is rather Bacchic.
A strophe of love.

JOB: (entering with Raphael) Where have you led me, young man?

RAPHAEL: Didn't I promise you a magnificent orgy?

JOB: Mein Gott! I feel myself eighty years younger. Look there, my young friend, see all those pretty women. Your wives, Nein! your divinities, your nymphs! (pointing to Euphrasie) That ravishing blonde.

RAPHAEL: (looking at him with pity, smiling) Poor, poor, fool!

RASTIGNAC: (standing, raising his glass) To the health of Raphael, our future editor-in-chief.

ALL: Bravo! Hail! (they drink)

RAPHAEL: Huh? What do I hear? (recognizing Rastignac) Rastignac?

GUILLAUME: What a shame, Mr. Rastignac, that your friend is not present at this party.

RASTIGNAC: What do you want? I looked for him in every corner of Paris. I'll find him again, don't worry, Papa Guillaume, even if I have to post up a reward for him.

RAPHAEL: (advancing into the middle of the hall) What's this folly signify?

RASTIGNAC: Raphael! Eh, by Jove! There he is, that dear friend.

ALL: (leaving their seats, surrounding Raphael) Long live Mr. Raphael.

GUILLAUME: (approaching Raphael and offering his hand) Sir, I am indeed honored, certainly—I am charmed.

RAPHAEL: (to Rastignac) Who's this imbecile?

RASTIGNAC: (low) Hush! Mr. Guillaume, former furrier, rich to millions, very distinguished statesman, who wants to be an ambassador. Greetings, Mr. Guillaume. (Guillaume bows) For the moment, the founder and provider of funds for a new paper: *The Scorpion* of which I've proclaimed you editor-in-chief. (turning towards the guests) Hurrah, for our editor-in-chief.

ALL: Long live the editor-in-chief!

RASTIGNAC: (giving a full glass to Raphael) Welcome to *The Scorpion*.

RAPHAEL: (aside) The Devil with it! Long live folly, dammit. I've lived as an anchorite long enough. (to guests) Thanks, my friends, thanks! and pour, pour a full glass. I intend to find, in intoxication, the balm that cures all the wounds of the heart.

RASTIGNAC: As for me, I'm taking charge of the scientific side; accounts paid for academic sessions, reviews of hospitals, medical dosages, the exposition of systems, allopathic, homeopathic, magnetism, hydrotherapy (presenting several guests to him successively) Mr. Lanternet, former traveling salesman for native sugar. Expansion, commerce, political economy, industrial statistics, market prices, audits and tariffs. Albert Tartereau, author of a vaudeville hissed at Bobino. Critical review of theatres. The *Courrier of Paris* belongs by right to the elegant Vicomte de Rancy.

RAPHAEL: De Rancy!

RASTIGNAC: Eh! By Jove! you know each other. One of your numerous rivals. The hottest worshiper—after you, of the beautiful Foedora.

RAPHAEL: Foedora! Don't pronounce that name.

RASTIGNAC: Why not? I am giving you my widow, you know, my Alsatian who reads Klopstock. Quarreled to death. I discovered she has six toes on her left foot. I cannot live with a woman who has six toes—that's ridiculous! And then she has only 20,000 francs income. Her fortune is diminishing as her toes increase. To the Devil with her, I'd do better to love Foedora.

RAPHAEL: (aside) Foedora! ah, forget her! forget her! (aloud) to table, gentlemen, to table.

ALL: To table! (each taking his place)

EUPHRASIE: (who's just noticed Job in a corner where he's been trying to hide, drags him by the arm into the middle of the room, laughing uproariously) Make way, gentlemen, make way for a living phenomenon.

JOB: (struggling) Mein Gott! You dislocating me—the beautiful girl. (general burst of laughter)

RASTIGNAC: In what Mummy's box did you unearth this old curiosity?

JOB: (indignant) Old curiosity!

RAPHAEL: (clapping Job on the back) Master Job, a well of science, gentlemen, a ton of gold, ladies. His old overcoat is lined with banknotes, his bedroom is paved with ingots and diamonds. With all that, generous like a Mexican, prodigal like a son of the family.

ALL THE WOMEN: (pushing around Job) Over here, Mr. Job. Mr. Job, here's a seat—beside me, Mr. Job.

EUPHRASIE: (grasping Job) One moment, one moment, ladies. He's mine. I found Mr. Job. I'm keeping him, don't be offended. (making him sit beside her)

RAPHAEL: (aside) Oh—the power of gold.

JOB: (sitting next to Euphrasie) She can be charming, this little girl.

RAPHAEL: Drink up, drink up again. And in the biggest glass. I have an arrears to complete. (a lady fills his glass which he empties, time after time, cup after cup)

RASTIGNAC: Keep pouring, Aquilina. Let it rise to our water level, to the Devil with wisdom! Long live joy, long live folly, long live wine. Right, Papa Guillaume?

GUILLAUME: I think like you, Mr. Rastignac.

EUPHRASIE: (continuing a conversation begun in a low voice) I assure you, you have the appearance of a young man.

JOB: (kissing her hand) The heart never ages.

RAPHAEL: Ah! I feel better.—Good wine! joyous companions, pretty girls. Hug me, Rastignac!

RASTIGNAC: (pushing Aquilina into his arms) By proxy, old boy!

RAPHAEL: Rastignac! You are a king. You are a god. When I am rich, I will pay your debts.

RASTIGNAC: Worthy friend! You hear him, ladies and gentlemen. I want witnesses.

RAPHAEL: But, what am I saying? I am rich—rich to millions.

RASTIGNAC: If you're not a millionaire, you are most certainly drunk.

RAPHAEL: Drunk with power! I can kill you. I am Nero, Nebuchadnezzar. My life has been a long silence. I intend to avenge myself on the whole world. I won't amuse myself by dissipating filthy lucre, I will consume human lives and minds. And souls. Now there's a luxury that's not cheap. It's the opulence of the plague. I will wrestle for power with yellow fever, blue fever, green fever, and with armies and all the plagues! I can be loved by Foedora!

DE RANCY: (rising) Sir, you will give me satisfaction!

RAPHAEL: Why, no! I don't want Foedora. She's my illness, Foedora! De Rancy, I am giving you Foedora.

RASTIGNAC: If you continue to shout I'll take you to the antechamber.

RAPHAEL: (pulling his talisman from his pocket and brandishing it with an air of triumph) You see this skin? It's the will of Solomon! Its mine; I own Arabia, Petra, even the Universe is mine! Mine! (to Rastignac) You are mine if I wish it. Ah, if I wish it! I can purchase your whole scientific shop, watch out! Your untouched scalpel, your imaginary patients, you will be my valet, and you will work like clock work.

RASTIGNAC: I will be your valet, that's agreed, but some manners, some decency. What the Devil! You are editor-in-chief. Do you love me?

RAPHAEL: Yes, I love you, dear friend! (hugs him)

RASTIGNAC: (to the guests) Is he sweet, huh?

RAPHAEL: Listen, this skin shrinks when I have a wish. Ask Master Job.

JOB: It's terrifying! The Devil!

RAPHAEL: You are going to see. Let's measure it. (calling) Waiter! (a waiter appears) Ink, a pen. (waiter leaves) Ah, no one believes me. We are going to laugh! (the waiter returns with writing materials) A napkin! (he spreads the napkin on the table and traces the peau de chagrin on it)

EUPHRASIE: (low to Job) Everyday, I go to the Tuileries.

JOB: (kissing her hand) Adorable!

RAPHAEL: The whole universe is contained in this shape. Now listen, in an hour, what do I say! before five minutes, I want to have 200,000 pounds of income.

RASTIGNAC: (forcing him to sit down) You will have them. Now sleep. Would you like a pillow?

RAPHAEL: Goodnight, illustrious doctor. You will amuse me, you will chase my flies away, and I will give you Havana cigars. (sleeps)

RASTIGNAC: Goodnight!

A WAITER: (entering, to Raphael) Sir, there's a notary who asks to speak to Mr. Raphael.

ALL: A notary!

RASTIGNAC: A notary. (waking Raphael) Eh! Raphael; do you hear? A notary wishes to speak to you.

RAPHAEL: A notary. Let this notary come! Hey! hey! waiter, a glass for the notary. (the waiter leaves)

RASTIGNAC: What's this signify? Do you understand, Papa Guillaume?

GUILLAUME: Not at all, Mr. Rastignac.

NOTARY: (entering, going straight to Raphael) Mr. Raphael.

RAPHAEL: Oh! oh! You know me?

NOTARY: Perfectly. Wasn't your mother a Miss O'Flaherty?

RAPHAEL: Yes. Barbara Marie Charlotte O'Flaherty. Born at Tours.

NOTARY: Well, sir. You are the sole and only heir of Major Martin O'Flaherty who died in August 1828, in Calcutta. The inheritance amounts to six millions, free and clear, ready money and liquid. (resting a portfolio on the table) Here's the first installment.

(Everyone rises in tumult. Raphael stands up, as if pushed by a spring, pale, emaciated, placing his hand on his heart as if he'd just received a wound.)

RASTIGNAC: What's the matter with him? How pale he is!

JOB: The talisman!

RAPHAEL: Yes! The Talisman! (he convulsively extends the peau de chagrin on the napkin where he traced its outline; he draws back in horror, uttering a scream)

RASTIGNAC: What do you see there?

RAPHAEL: (extending his hand towards the talisman) Death! death!

RASTIGNAC: (looking at the table) Indeed. That peau de chagrin has shrunk.

ALL: (going to the table and leaning over to look) Let's see, Let's see.

(Rastignac rises in a manner so that the audience can see the talisman extended on the napkin doesn't reach the contours traced by Raphael)

RAPHAEL: (abruptly seizing the peau de chagrin) Get back! Get back! All you who made me lose my reason. Wretches! You've killed me. (everyone shrinks back exclaiming in fear and pity) Rich to millions—and dying. (falls, overwhelmed into his chair)

RASTIGNAC: (low to Guillaume) What do you say to all this, Papa Guillaume?

GUILLAUME: I say!—whatever you please, Mr. Rastignac.

RASTIGNAC: (to Raphael who remains silent as if annihilated) Well, what? Have you died suddenly because a six million brick landed on your head? Courage, what the Devil, and do me justice! (hands him his glass)

RAPHAEL: (making a violent effort to control himself) Well said, dammit! and to the Devil with dark thoughts! (calling) Waiter! Bring the whole wine cellar up here.

CHORUS: Children of folly, etc.

CURTAIN

ACT III

SCENE IV

For the Poor, If You Please

A lighted garden. Music can be heard off throughout the act. Numerous groups circulate at the back of the stage, so that the stage is never left completely empty. All the women are in costumes and masked. There are only several men. Raphael, Rastignac and de Rancy enter dressed in town clothes.

RAPHAEL: (offering his hand to Rastignac) I am happy to see you my old friend, my old comrade—and it was a good idea you had to write me to come to this ball.

RASTIGNAC: It was, indeed, necessary to resort to this means since the door to your hotel is locked, bolted and padlocked like the gate to a fortress. For the last three months I've been seeking you in every corner of Paris. Disappeared, eclipsed. I thought you were dead. Yesterday, at last, I noticed you in the Champs Elysees. I was on horseback. Ten minutes of galloping and I arrived in time to see you at the door of your hotel. I asked for Mr. Raphael. The Swiss guard, a real Swiss, by Jove, answered me: "Dunno! This hotel belongs to the Marquis de Filegraine." "Go for the Marquis de Villecraisnes," I replied. But Bah! impossible to penetrate further. "Duh Marquis dozn't receive anybuddy," your Cerberus told me.

RAPHAEL: That's true; but that instruction is not for you, and if I'd known—

RASTIGNAC: Great! But, at least tell me the reason for this unbelievable seclusion? Pass to former times when you were stopping up holes in the door of your garret in the Hotel Saint Quentin to gnaw your crusts in hiding.

RAPHAEL: Ah, my friend, those were the good times.

RASTIGNAC: Are you making fun of me? The good times! You were going to throw yourself in the river.

RAPHAEL: Oh, then, I had nothing which could make

me love life, while now—

RASTIGNAC: Well?

RAPHAEL: (placing himself in front of him) How do I look to you?

RASTIGNAC: What do you mean?

RAPHAEL: Look at these dull eyes, this faded face, these emaciated hands. Do you think I have a long time to live?

RASTIGNAC: No, if you obstinately continue to lead this snail's life; yes, if you wish to amuse yourself, distract yourself. You have the spleen. Kill it, if you don't want it to kill you. Why not enjoy your fortune? What use are your millions to you? You wanted to be rich.

RAPHAEL: I don't want anything, now.

RASTIGNAC: Even to make the beautiful Foedora love you? To destroy her, as you said, with all the weight of your luxury, to dazzle her with the glitter of your fortune and your glory?

RAPHAEL: Foedora! I don't even know if I loved that

woman!

RASTIGNAC: Plague! You've got a short memory. In your place I should have wanted—

RAPHAEL: Wanted—for me to want what may be in this world! Why, have you forgotten that each of my wants, each of my caprices is one more step towards the grave? (pulling from his pocket the peau de chagrin) Have you forgotten the murderous characters of this fatal talisman?

RASTIGNAC: Your peau de chagrin. Why, do you seriously believe in this plaything?

RAPHAEL: Yes, I believe in it! But, wretch! Don't you recall that wish for riches that I formed one day and the marvelous rapidity with which it was realized?

RASTIGNAC: Fine—fortuitous coincidence, pure chance!

RAPHAEL: Chance, also, right, the swift shrinking of this membrane? You saw it, I measured it in front of you.

RASTIGNAC: You were drunk and so was I. We had

trouble seeing it.

RAPHAEL: Skeptic and scoffer! You can do that without danger. But as for me, you see, I, who pay for every thought with a piece of myself, I shiver at all times of the day at the least tremor of this terrible talisman. The peau de chagrin is like a tiger with whom I must live without awakening its ferocity.

RASTIGNAC: (touching his face with the tips of his fingers) Poor friend. There's your tiger. There's your executioner!

RAPHAEL: You think I'm crazy? Yes, that must be it. But you cannot cure me. So let's leave that! What are you doing? What's become of you?

RASTIGNAC: The Scorpion's dead.

RAPHAEL: Ah!

RASTIGNAC: Our capitalist, Papa Guillaume, was a coward; didn't he have the audacity to demand the books?

RAPHAEL: The insolent!

RASTIGNAC: We sent him the memoirs of Vefour and Tortoni. Vulgar fellow, got all red and angry. Goodbye the subsidy. To end it, I am getting married.

RAPHAEL: With your Alsatian?

RASTIGNAC: Still, even though I discovered she only possesses 10,000 francs income. It's true she still has six toes on her left foot. That's a compensation. Only, as she is jealous, and idleness is, according to Klopstock, the source of all conjugal misery, she insists that I find an occupation for myself.

RAPHAEL: And what are you going to do?

RASTIGNAC: I've solicited and obtained a job. Doctor inspector of the waters of Mont Dore! Six thousand francs a year income to be made. I am the man of the place. I am leaving in a week, right after my marriage. You ought to come with me. You need some air, motion, distraction.

RAPHAEL: Perhaps you're right. I will think about it. I feel myself reviving already in this atmosphere of festivity and pleasure.

RASTIGNAC: Do you want to take a tour in the ballroom?

RAPHAEL: Willingly.

(They go upstage. Gertrau, who's just entered from the back, thanks a mask with whom she's been dancing, and latches on to the arms of Rastignac. Raphael moves toward the back but never leaves the stage.)

RASTIGNAC: (to Gertrau, who is wearing a Hungarian costume) My darling, Gertrau. If I had less love for you, I would tell you that you are unsupportable, I allowed you to come to this ball in the hope of amusing you, of tearing you away temporarily from your whining Teutonics, and, hardly on my arm, you utter heartbreaking moans.

GERTRAU: Why did you make me to wear this costume? It reminds me of the misfortunes of Poland.

RASTIGNAC: Great. Now, its politics and foreign politics. It wasn't enough with Jean Paul, Goethe, and with Klopstock. I warn you, my darling, that when we are married, in place of philosophical books I will only allow you the novels of Paul de Kock. You are becoming too lugubrious, word of honor. (To Raphael who comes forward to them) Ah, dear fellow, there you are! (to

Gertrau) The Marquis Raphael de Villecraisnes, my best friend. (Gertrau and Raphael bow to each other) (to Raphael) The Baroness Swiebelaugen, who will, I hope, soon exchange her harsh name for the more harmonious moniker of Rastignac. (pointing to de Rancy who advances toward them) Eh, why, look at Rancy will you. Doesn't he seem like a soul in pain?

DE RANCY: (accosting them) Good evening, gentlemen. (bowing to Gertrau) Are you enjoying yourself?

RASTIGNAC: I enjoy myself everywhere.

GERTRAU: As for me, I bore myself everywhere.

RASTIGNAC: Much obliged! (to de Rancy) What's happened to you this evening?

DE RANCY: My God, I wouldn't have said this in front of Raphael three months ago. He would surely have cut our throats. But now he's no longer concerned about Foedora

RASTIGNAC: Ah! It's a question of Foedora?

RAPHAEL: So you're still amorous, my poor de Rancy?

DE RANCY: More than ever. I'm losing my head over her, if I haven't already. So, imagine that this morning the beautiful Countess begged me to accompany her to this ball. A masked ball. That is to say, freedom from censure; isolation in the midst of a crowd. Judge my happiness. I thought of nothing else all day. Finally, to-night, I rushed to her hotel. I found her stretched on a couch. Sulky. In an execrable humor. She had a headache. Do you understand? A headache on the day of a ball. In short, she refused to get dressed. I wanted to remain with her. She told me she needed to rest. In a word, she put me out the door.

RASTIGNAC: (shaking his hand affectionately) Poor friend!

RAPHAEL: (taking his other hand) I know that! more so than you, my dear de Rancy. I acquired through cruel experience a deep knowledge of the heart of women. Know one thing, my dear friend. It's that Foedora will be at this ball tonight.

DE RANCY: Despite her headache?

RAPHAEL: Because of her headache.

DE RANCY: The affirmation is pointed. And I confess I

would be curious to see—

RAPHAEL: (pointing to a white domino that has just appeared at the back and seems to be looking for someone) Look!

DE RANCY: Indeed, it's her figure, her shape.

RAPHAEL: (aside) It sufficed me to will it and my will was fulfilled. Yet another step towards death. But, at least, I will be avenged on this woman.

DE RANCY: Ah, by Jove! I will teach her she cannot play this way with a gallant man.

FOEDORA: (coming forward rapidly and going straight to Raphael, saying with astonishment) Raphael!

RAPHAEL: The most devoted of your admirers, Countess, but you didn't expect to meet me at this ball?

FOEDORA: Yes. A secret premonition. Oh! I am very happy not to have fought it.

RAPHAEL: (to de Rancy) You hear her?

DE RANCY: And your migraine, Countess?

FOEDORA: (haughtily) I took you to be a man of the world, Mr. de Rancy. (she turns to Rastignac and talks to him in a low voice)

DE RANCY: As for me, I thought—Madame—

RAPHAEL: (interrupting him) Shut up; this woman is not worthy of your rage, she was playing with you, as she would play again with me.

DE RANCY: I don't want to believe you.

RAPHAEL: Watch and judge her. (de Rancy moves away, as does Rastignac, but without losing sight of Foedora and Raphael) (taking Foedora's hand) And I, too, I was expecting you. And I, also, had a premonition that I would see you this evening.

FOEDORA: What became of you for the last three months?

RAPHAEL: Oh—I was very unhappy.

FOEDORA: Unhappy! Aren't you rich now? Rich to millions?

RAPHAEL: (low to de Rancy who passes near him and who has heard these last words) Do you understand now why she had a migraine? (to Foedora) Is fortune all there is to happiness? Foedora, you were really cruel, really implacable to me. Do you know that your disdain made me want to die?

FOEDORA: To die?

RAPHAEL: (observing her) To die, yes! More than once, I invoked death. One day, amidst others. I did it under your eyes. A cruel death. A hideous death. One step more and—

FOEDORA: (smiling) Oh! That step is always the most difficult to take.

RAPHAEL: (repressing a gesture of indignation) In stopping myself at the edge of the abyss, doubtless, I injured your glory.

FOEDORA: (aside) So bitter! He still loves me. (aloud) Child! Who pushed you to that act of folly? Kill oneself—over a woman's caprice? Who? You, a scientist, a philosopher. You, who have plumbed the depths of the human heart! Are you unaware that love, vanquished, but ashamed of its defeat, sometimes takes the appearance of hate, and that, like savage warriors, in giving up its last breath, insults the enemy again. It's for the injury, it's for the outrage, that modesty avenges itself as it succumbs.

RAPHAEL: (after signaling de Rancy to approach without Foedora's noticing) What! When you were taking pleasure in torturing me, ripping my heart out—you loved me?

FOEDORA: Instead of fleeing me, after that cruel scene, if you'd returned to me, perhaps, you would have learned.

RAPHAEL: (fixing his glance on Foedora) Come to the point!

FOEDORA: What's the good? Why evoke a vanished past? Why stir up these ill extinguished ashes?

RAPHAEL: Foedora! You loved me!

FOEDORA: (pretending embarrassment) Raphael—don't question me!

RAPHAEL: (taking the hidden hand of de Rancy) You loved me! Oh, fool that I was! Why did I have to doubt you. That my outbursts, my violence had offended you forever, perhaps! You are silent. Don't ravish the hope you've just given me! Foedora, answer me now, now, once more: do you love me?

FOEDORA: (leaning towards him, in a passionate voice) And, if I tell you: yes!

RAPHAEL: (standing abruptly) Well, I will tell you: you're lying!

FOEDORA: (recoiling) What do I hear (noticing de Rancy, and Rastignac, who rushes up because of Raphael's explosive voice) Ah! They are listening to us.

RAPHAEL: Ah, that astonishes you! You cannot believe that this man, who was your slave, your dog,—who, to obtain one smile, that he never did obtain, whose pride, whose honor, whose dignity, you soiled under your feet! You cannot believe that this man, who wanted to kill himself for you, the imbecile! has developed a heart of marble like yours, and that your cajoleries, your studied sighs, your knowing winks, amuse him now, as they amused you, as you would be again amused by his cries of rage and despair! Ah! you are still a coquette, Countess. Well, as for me, I've become stupid!

FOEDORA: Fool! You said it just now! Now you are one. Wretch. You no longer believe in love.

RAPHAEL: (slowly, penetrating) Yes! I believe in love that purifies hearts instead of corrupting them! in love, the source of all sacrifices, all devotion, all immolation! in love which is happy in its anguish, love which out-lives ingratitude, love that smiles when it weeps! That type of love, wretch that I am! That pure love, that chaste love, that devoted love, that I inspired and that I did not recognize. Poor Pauline! poor child who loved me like a murmuring stream, like a singing bird. Be-cause that love is an instinct, a need of your heart. Oh, how you will be avenged by my disdain, if you learn what rival I preferred to you!

FOEDORA: (laughing) Ah, ah, ah. The word is charm-ing. You see me as a rival of Miss Pauline!

RAPHAEL: Know this well. It's to her the rivalry is a shame.

FOEDORA: Miss Pauline. Some suspect and interesting orphan; some learned and unappreciated grisette.

RAPHAEL: And you, who are you? For in the end, who knows you? Where are your guarantees? Where is your warrantor? Once more, who are you? Where did you get your name? your title? your fortune? Who even knows where you come from? or from where you came?

FOEDORA: Sir, this is too much!

RAPHAEL: Don't the mysteries of your life legitimatize every suspicion? An orphan, you say? Since when is misfortune a title of shame? A working girl? Well, Madame, below working girls there is a place for courtesans.

FOEDORA: (raging) Such an outrage—

RAPHAEL: Ah, you speak of others! Well, I intend to know who you are. (to maskers who fill the back of the stage) and what you are. Come forward, come forward! By Jove, it's a surprise reserved for us by the Master of Ceremonies of these festivities, a scene of white magic! On my soul, this will be curious.

FOEDORA: What's he going to do?

RAPHAEL: It's the story of a woman that you are all going to know. (He points to a wall of shrubs; the shrubs separate and reveal an animated picture revealing a woman wretchedly dressed. This woman plays an organ placed on small cart, in which is placed a child in swaddling clothes lying on a straw litter.)

ALL: This is charming! This is charming!

FOEDORA: (stupefied) My mother! Where am I? What is this prodigy?

RAPHAEL: (laughing) Your mother! That poor beggar woman is your mother? It was you who said it, Foedora! And without doubt, this child in swaddling clothes—it's you. (the tableau vanishes)

FOEDORA: (aside) By what infernal power?

RASTIGNAC: (to de Rancy) Masterfully contrived, by Jove! But how was he able to know —?

RAPHAEL: Now, do you want to see yourself as a young girl? (A new tableau appears; it represents a young girl of fifteen, covered with rags, holding in front of her a basket filled with bouquets. A Russian General, in a fine uniform, takes a bouquet from the smiling girl. The General caresses the young girl's chin, while a Cossack places a cashmere over her shoulders.)

ALL: (applauding) Bravo! Bravo!

FOEDORA: (aside) Good God!

RAPHAEL: You were pretty, you know, at fifteen. Despite those frightful rags, and this Russian General was a connoisseur, my word. I divine it all now; after the retreat of the Armies of the Holy Alliance, your seducer led you to Moscow—where you made a fortune! Ah, it's a great country, Russia!

FOEDORA: (starting up before Raphael with a scream of rage) Ah, if you are not a demon, you are the most cowardly of men! (to Rastignac) Mr. de Rastignac, a gallant man owes protection to all women. (pointing to Raphael who laughs) If you are a man of heart, you will avenge me on this wretch.

RASTIGNAC: Raphael is my friend, Madame.

FOEDORA: (to de Rancy) But you, Hector. He is your enemy; he was your rival.

DE RANCY: (coldly) I am no longer jealous, Madame.

FOEDORA: I was wrong, gentlemen. One doesn't ask protection except from people one esteems. Destitute as you think me, know well, that a woman like me never lacks defenders. (to Raphael) Man or Demon, bad luck to you! (she is lost in the crowd which disperses right and left)

DE RANCY: I was stupid. It was as if being under the influence of an infernal charm.

RASTIGNAC: It's disenchantment which is operating. De Rancy, my friend, you must amuse yourself, distract yourself, take a tour of the ball with my wife. She's very gay, very frolicsome, she will make you laugh.

GERTRAU: (low) Are you crazy?

RASTIGNAC: Two minutes only. I have to speak to Raphael.

DE RANCY: (offering his arm to Gertrau) I am happy, Madame, if you'd be willing to accept—

GERTRAU: (taking his arm) Through obedience, sir. For I warn you, I feel like crying tonight.

DE RANCY: (to Rastignac who watches him, laughing) Ah! Traitor! (leaves with Gertrau)

RASTIGNAC: Bravo! Bravo! my friend! Your magic

scene was admirable, and the Count will be jealous of your talent. But, how were you able to know the mysteries of this woman's life?

RAPHAEL: Through the power of my will.

RASTIGNAC: (laughing) What—you want me to believe?

RAPHAEL: That scene was not a play! That scene was reality—

RASTIGNAC: Come on! Still, your fixed idea!

RAPHAEL: You saw Foedora's rage.

RASTIGNAC: Yes, but I also heard her threats of vengeance. Take care, Raphael, that woman is capable of anything.

RAPHAEL: Bah! Don't I know that my life is sheltered from all attacks, and that nothing in the world can put me in peril so long as a patch of the talisman remains with me?

RASTIGNAC: (aside, touching his forehead with the tip of his finger to indicate that Raphael is mad) Always his terrifying hobby horse. (they leave, talking, by the left)

(Job and Euphrasie come in. Euphrasie is on his arm, in the costume of a southern peasant. They are surrounded by a group of masks who are laughing at them. Job is disguised as a troubadour, a plume in his cap, mandolin on his back, swinging about and aping the grace of a young man.)

HAMILCAR: (disguised as an old soldier of the Empire, to the crowd) Oh! children—who is it who lost his grandfather? (pointing to Job) There's an ancestor, all revived, perfumed, curled, pomaded like a cherubim. A love of Methuselah himself. Speak friends, pay your court. (they laugh)

JOB: (struggling with himself) Will you leave me in peace? Der Teufel!

HAMILCAR: Return home, little scamp, you'll get a whipping from your mother.

JOB: Don't come near me, Mein Gott!

HAMILCAR: (to the crowd) A hot one! A sugared treat for little fan-fan!

JOB: (getting angry) Back. Philistines! Amalikites! Sons of Gomorrah!

EUPHRASIE: (waving the crowd off with a gesture) Ah, this is annoying in the end. Aren't there any police here? One cannot circulate peacefully with one's chevalier.

HAMILCAR: Her chevalier. Oho! Her Mummy!

JOB: A mummy!

EUPHRASIE: A mummy! That's not true. He's a man and a young man still!

JOB: (triumphant) You hear! a young man. (to Euphrasie) Tomorrow, I'll buy you a carriage.

HAMILCAR: She's getting angry, La Peasant Girl. Oho! Friends, ring around these turtle doves.

ALL: Bravo! Bravo! Long live Hamilcar!

(All the Maskers join hands and ring around Job and Euphrasie, singing. The orchestra plays a tune. Job, agitated like one possessed, in the middle of the circle, rushes to Raphael who is returning with Rastignac.)

JOB: I am dead, murdered! Ah! The scoundrels! The sons of Belial.

RAPHAEL: Calm down Master Job.

JOB: (recognizing him) Mr. Raphael. Ah, protect me, defend me. (looking around him) Euphrasie—where is Euphrasie?

EUPHRASIE: (running up) Here I am, my friend.

JOB: (kissing her hand) Dear little hand. (a waltz can be heard off)

HAMILCAR: (separating from the crowd) A waltz. Move aside, gang. (to Job) Goodbye, old troubadour of my heart. (a group of masks leaves, waltzing)

RAPHAEL: (to Job) Do you know, you don't look twenty, Master Job?

JOB: Don't I? Oh! Love—it's the true fountain of youth.

EUPHRASIE: Don't make him talk too much. On account of his catarrh.

JOB: (to Raphael, pressing his hand) Mr. Raphael. you are an angel, a god! Before knowing you, I lived like a mollusk, like an oyster. I've wasted a hundred years of my life, Mr. Raphael. But you see, I am recapturing them.

RAPHAEL: Still amorous, Master Job?

JOB: (looking shrewdly at Euphrasie who lowers her eyes modestly) Ask the little woman!

RASTIGNAC: A pretty girl, by Jove! (looking in the distance) And if I were sure that Gertrau—

JOB'S CLERK: (entering excitedly) Master Job! ah! At last I've found you! Since this morning, when you left the shop to run I don't know where, some fine things have happened.

JOB: (turning quickly) Huh! What—What's he want with me? I am in company—

RAPHAEL: Don't trouble yourself, Master Job. (he crosses the stage looking from one side to the other)

CLERK: Can I have two words with you?

JOB: Two, not more. Euphrasie, wait for me, my sweetie. (moving away a few steps with his clerk)

RASTIGNAC: (to Euphrasie) Wouldn't you like to take a tour of the ball, my charmer?

EUPHRASIE: Only a minute. (pointing to Job) He is so jealous. (they leave by the side)

JOB: Well! Did lightning strike the shop?

CLERK: Worse than that, boss. The Bailiffs.

JOB: The Bailiffs—Mein Gott!

CLERK: Everything's been seized. In a week, everything will be sold.

JOB: Well! The merchandise was made to be sold.

CLERK: But wake up, boss. Don't you understand. Today, the seizure. In a week, the sale. In a month. Clichy.

JOB: Clichy. Understand perfectly. Clichy. There will be so much Champagne there. Euphrasie will come to me tonight. (turning, looking for her) Euphrasie. Where is Euphrasie?

CLERK: (taking Job by the arm) One more word, boss.

JOB: (getting loose) Go to the Devil! I must find Euphrasie. (running out)

CLERK: Is this really Master Job? (running off after him)

RAPHAEL: (coming forward, watching Job) Go, cursed old man. Trample under your foot, your wisdom of which you were so proud. Cast to the wind your millions, you were so avaricious of.—After all, he's happy. Whereas I—(he remains for a moment, then Fedora appears in the distance with Hamilcar, leaning on his shoulder, pointing to Raphael)

HAMILCAR: (to Foedora) That pale little thing? Why, I will kill him with my little finger; he's got no more strength than a midge. (gesture of impatience from Foedora) In the end, my all-beautiful, you wish it. I promised, and I keep my word. But think as well, that I will remind you of your promise. Tomorrow, you will come to lunch with me. (Foedora gives him her bouquet and sneaks out) That's good. Agreed. (Coming forward and planting himself directly in front of Raphael. At this point all the characters return to the stage and slowly group around Raphael and Hamilcar.)

HAMILCAR: (to Raphael) Sir!

RAPHAEL: (turning) What do you want?

HAMILCAR: You stepped on my foot just now.

RAPHAEL: It's possible in the midst of the crowd. I am vexed over it.

HAMILCAR: I think, also, you looked askance at me.

RAPHAEL: It's probably because I wasn't facing you.

HAMILCAR: That's an insult, sir.

RAPHAEL: Do you think so? In that case, receive my excuses.

HAMILCAR: (aside) The Devil! (aloud) I don't accept them, sir.

RAPHAEL: (turning his back) In that case, go to the Devil!

RASTIGNAC: (entering with Euphrasie and going quickly to Raphael) What's the matter? A quarrel?

RAPHAEL: (smiling) No, a joke. (pointing to Hamilcar) The gentleman's amusing himself.

HAMILCAR: Sir, I take it upon myself to teach you one thing. It's that your face displeases the whole company here, and me, in particular.

RAPHAEL: (to Rastignac) You see, this gentleman is playing his part. A braggart, revived from the Empire.

JOB: (entering and noticing Euphrasie on Rastignac's arm) Euphrasie, nice behavior.

EUPHRASIE: (taking his arm and pointing to Hamilcar) Hush! a dispute!

HAMILCAR: A pale and ghastly face like a cotton cap— that gets on my nerves. Go to bed; you are ill.

RAPHAEL: Where did you study medicine?

HAMILCAR: Sir, I received my bachelors with Lepage and my licentiate with Bertrand.

JOB: (approaching Hamilcar) Enough, young man! enough. Any more and you'll have to fight with the

Devil!

HAMILCAR: (pushing him away) Ah, silence, old urchin.

RAPHAEL: (gravely) That man spoke the truth, sir. If I support your provocations and insults with patience, it's because I like to be generous, and because I don't wish to punish too cruelly the stupidity of a youth. I possess a terrible power, I warn you of it; you are doubtless counting on your competence as a swashbuckler. Well to annihilate your skill, to veil your eyes, to make your hands tremble and your heart palpitate, even to kill you, sir—all I have to do is wish it.

HAMILCAR: Charming! charming! Do you think you can frighten me with your old wives' tales?

RAPHAEL: Well, sir, since you absolutely must have a lesson, you shall receive it. But, I want some other than myself to administer it to you. (looking around and noticing Job) This gentleman, for example.

JOB: Me!

RAPHAEL: Yes, you will fight with this gentleman.

JOB: (hiding behind Raphael) With me, Mein Gott!

HAMILCAR: Sonofabitch! I know how to force you. (He raises his hand to strike Raphael, but Raphael gestures and the blow falls on Job's cheek. Bursts of laughter from the crowd.)

JOB: (rushing on Hamilcar) Your weapons, der Teufel!

HAMILCAR: (pushing Job away) Go take a stroll.

JOB: You struck me! I have the right to kill you, der Teufel!

EUPHRASIE: (trying to calm him) My little friend.

JOB: (furious) Leave me alone, dammit!

VOICES IN THE CROWD: He's right! He's been insulted.

HAMILCAR: What! You want me to fight with this old nutcracker!

JOB: (getting up) This old nutcracker has a good foot, a good eye, and he will prove it to you, by Jove. Let's go, sir.

HAMILCAR: Now?

JOB: (proudly) A duel by torchlight. That's like the Regency. Mr. Rastignac. You be my witness.

RASTIGNAC: Willingly, Master Job. (aside) By God, I am curious to see this fight.

HAMILCAR: (laughing) Come on, this will be funny.

(Job and Hamilcar leave, followed by Rastignac and several masks. The others continue to stroll about at the back.)

RAPHAEL: (seated on a grass bench) All this uproar bores and tires me. What! It's not enough my life is rushing like a torrent, and that my shortened days are flowing by with the rapidity of hours. Must the little time, that remains to me to live, be poisoned by cares and continual terrors! Ah, only a strong passion, only love can halt the decay of my soul! Love, ah, if it can rejuvenate an old imbecile, it will know well enough how to restore my vanished vigor and my lost happiness! Pauline, dear and noble child, who laughed with my joy, who wept my tears, Pauline, oh, my sweet guardian angel! It's you I want to love. It's you who will bring back my soul, and all the joys, all the enchantments of my youth. Return to me, Pauline, as I return to you. A smile to your lips, love in your heart. (At the end of this speech, Pauline in a white muslin robe, without a mask, accompanied by a grey mustached old man, who wears decorations, comes slowly forward from the back, hiding her face from the public. Reaching Raphael who hasn't noticed her, she presents him with a purse.)

PAULINE: For the poor if you please!

RAPHAEL: (stupefied) Pauline!

PAULINE: (trembling with emotion) Mr. Raphael.

RAPHAEL: Is this a dream?

PAULINE: (pointing to the masks who observe her) They're looking at us.

RAPHAEL: Well, tomorrow, at your mother's. At the Hotel Saint Quentin.

PAULINE: (leaves without responding, to various masks, repeatedly) For the poor if you please.

RAPHAEL: (following her with his eyes) At the Hotel Saint-Quentin. It's there that I met her, Yes, yes, I will go to this rendezvous.

(A great tumult at the rear. Masks rush forward with torches. Four wharf porters carry Job in triumph, shouting.)

WHARF PORTERS: Long live the troubadour.

(Job, crowned with flowers bows left and right. Racket of reed pipes and kestrels.)

CURTAIN

ACT IV

SCENE V

Hate and Love

Same as first scene.

RAPHAEL: (entering with Madame Gervais) So this hotel no longer belongs to Mrs. Gaudin?

MADAME GERVAIS: No, sir. For the last month. Oh! Madame Gaudin is a great lady now. She calls herself the Baroness.—I never can hammer that name in my head.

RAPHAEL: De Witschnaur.

MADAME GERVAIS: De Witschnaur; that's fine, that's

it. She has a carriage, servants, a big house for herself alone. Another near the water. She wears a bunch of diamonds at her throat. Real diamonds, big like ostrich eggs—ones that don't hurt the eyes to look at.

RAPHAEL: And, how do they say this fortune came to her?

MADAME GERVAIS: Quite honestly, sir. Her husband brought it to her; the poor, dear man. They hadn't heard news of him since the campaign in Russia. Everyone thought he was dead; except his wife, who said to whoever wanted to hear, that one of these fine mornings Papa Gaudin would come back from the Indies with thousands and hundreds, on account of she had dreamed of a ship full of serpents—Everyone laughed at her, the good woman. Now, she's laughing at the others.

RAPHAEL: Strange event.

MADAME GERVAIS: Ah, she's a good woman, all the same. She's no prouder today than she was yesterday. She gave me, for free, her grounds, and the remainder of her lease. She excepted from the gift only this room, which I have to keep for a year at the disposition of her former tenant.

RAPHAEL: (looking around him) It seems to me you haven't respected the will of your benefactress?

MADAME GERVAIS: Alas, my dear sir, the times are so harsh, and money so rare! And then they said you were dead and buried. I found a young man, a student, to rent it.

RAPHAEL: (pointing with the edge of his cane to a woman's bonnet thrown in the corner of the room) Ah! That's a young man?

MADAME GERVAIS: (picking up the bonnet and thrusting it in her pocket) Heavens! it's Cephise's bonnet. I will bring it to her, that dear sweetie.

RAPHAEL: Cephise. She's his mistress.

MADAME GERVAIS: Oh! He's a jolly fellow, that Mr. Hamilcar.

RAPHAEL: That's fine, but this room belongs to me, my dear Madame Gervais. And I expect Mr. Hamilcar to change his residence as soon as possible.

MADAME GERVAIS: He won't oppose it, he's such a nice kid, Mr. Hamilcar. I rented it to him only on condition. We indeed have one vacant. Heavens! someone's coming upstairs—if it were Mr. Hamilcar. (singing off) It's him. I recognize his voice.

HAMILCAR: (entering without seeing Raphael) It's you, Mrs. Gervais. Run! Go down. They're asking for you in the lodge (Hamilcar has his arm in a sling)

MADAME GERVAIS: Thanks, Mr. Hamilcar. I am going to leave you with this gentleman. (she exits)

HAMILCAR: (bowing to Raphael) Sir! (recognizing him) Heavens! The Pekinese from the masked ball.

RAPHAEL: That face. I'm not mistaken. It's you who, last night—

HAMILCAR: Provoked you—on the cheek of a terrible little troubadour. Well, my dear sir, the terrible troubadour put a ball in my arm, as you see; I don't know how he did it, for he was trembling as he was aiming at me.

RAPHAEL: Yes. That had to happen!

HAMILCAR: (serious) What do you mean it had to happen! Ah, indeed. Do you want to provoke me in your turn?

RAPHAEL: No, sir, that's not the motive for my visit. I am persuaded that you regret a moment of thoughtlessness.

HAMILCAR: Damn it, you're right! I was trying to find a German quarrel with you. What do you want? Champagne? Two pretty eyes? As for me, I've never been able to resist 'em!

RAPHAEL: Two pretty eyes! What do you mean?

HAMILCAR: Pretend innocence, farceur!

RAPHAEL: I assure you.

HAMILCAR: The little chick you allowed yourself to— (makes a sign of pinching a woman's behind) Bah! I don't wish you ill for that. If I had received a sword cut every time I—(repeating the gesture)

RAPHAEL: (astonished totally) What, a woman egged you on?

HAMILCAR: A woman. A beauty, ah!

RAPHAEL: (suddenly remembering) A white domino,

perhaps?

HAMILCAR: There you go. We've got it.

RAPHAEL: That woman, you know her?

HAMILCAR: (scowling) Hell!

RAPHAEL: You know her name, I mean?

HAMILCAR: Her name! She made me no mystery of that. Her name's Francine. The most ravishing grisette in the Latin Quarter.

RAPHAEL: (aside) Francine! a grisette—I'm lost. (aloud) Let's leave that, and talk, if you don't mind, of the business that brings me here.

HAMILCAR: If you'd like a seat, sir?

RAPHAEL: Thanks! I want to pray you, sir, to give me back this room.

HAMILCAR: Ah! Bah!

RAPHAEL: It belonged to me for a year, before I left this hotel, three months ago.

HAMILCAR: That's fair. Madame Gervais warned me. Heavens, heavens. That's you (pointing to some papers) on the desk—who took care to furnish my lights.

RAPHAEL: (examining the papers excitedly) What, sir, you burned them?

HAMILCAR: Used 'em to light my pipe! A philosophic treatise. Do you imagine I read it, by chance? Not so stup—(correcting himself politely) so indiscreet.

RAPHAEL: Indeed. For a few dreams the less, mankind won't sicken.

HAMILCAR: So, sir, it's agreed. I am returning your Louvre to you. The Devil! As for me, it's just that I don't know where to roost.

RAPHAEL: There's a vacant room in the hotel.

HAMILCAR: In that case! Forward, with all I have— (calling at the top of the stairs) Madame Gervais. Hey, hey, hey!

MADAME GERVAIS: (off) Huh? What's wrong?

HAMILCAR: A chariot and six horses for moving my household.

MADAME GERVAIS: That's good, wise guy!

RAPHAEL: (looking around him) That will be quick.

HAMILCAR: (unhooking an old fireman's helmet) All objects of luxury.

MADAME GERVAIS: (entering) At your orders, Mr. Hamilcar.

HAMILCAR: Carry it off, Mama. (Passing several worthless objects to her. Pipes, a candle in a bottle, an old guitar, a shirt collar.)

MADAME GERVAIS: That's all?

HAMILCAR: What do you mean, that's all? You think something is lacking? (to Raphael, who is staring out the window) Goodbye, neighbor! (Hamilcar leaves with Madame Gervais)

RAPHAEL: Goodbye, sir.

RAPHAEL: It's here she appeared to me for the first

time, with her childlike grace, with her sweet smile that so often healed the wounds of my heart. It seems to me I see her still, seated before this piano rehearsing with me the divine songs of our greatest masters. How smooth and pure her voice was! How it expressed every emotion, every tenderness in her soul. (letting himself fall into an armchair) Darling Pauline! She loved me! Yesterday, I read her love in the accent of her voice, in her troubled looks. She loved me, for she had guessed my secret. Poor child! How she must have suffered. Oh, I intend to return to her fivefold all the love my mad passion stole from her. I want her to forget, as I will myself forget, those funereal days in my life when, to run after a chimera, I drove off happiness which came before me by itself.

(Pauline enters in an expensive town dress. She approaches Paul noiselessly and leans over him in the armchair he is sitting in.)

PAULINE: Happiness has returned. Will you drive it away again?

RAPHAEL: Pauline! Oh, thanks for having come!

PAULINE: Did you doubt my word?

RAPHAEL: If I was told heaven was going to open before me, would doubting it be a crime?

PAULINE: You are pale! You've suffered.

RAPHAEL: Yes, I've been very unhappy.

PAULINE: There! I guessed that yesterday, seeing you dressed well. Rich in appearance and in reality, huh? Mr. Raphael, is it still like before?

RAPHAEL: No. I am rich. Very rich.

PAULINE: He's rich! What luck. You would have rejected me if you'd been poor. I know you, you are proud. (prying into his eyes) Eh, tell me, that woman?

RAPHAEL: That woman! I hate her, I scorn her. (pulling her towards him) Pauline, it's you. It's you alone, I love.

PAULINE: (ravished) He loves me! He loves me! Go! We will be happy! I am rich, too, my Raphael, To millions. You love luxury. But you must love my heart, also! There's so much love for you in my heart! You don't know? My father returned. It was he who gave me his arm at the ball. I am a rich heiress! My mother and father are leaving me entirely free to choose my fate. I am free, free, you understand? (confused) Pardon. I don't know how such boldness came over me.

RAPHAEL: Boldness. My pardon? Oh, don't be afraid. It's love, true love, deep, eternal, like mine, right?

PAULINE: Oh, speak! speak! Your mouth has been mute for me too long!

RAPHAEL: You loved me then?

PAULINE: Oh God! Yes, I loved you! Go, Raphael; by offering you my heart, my person, my fortune, I won't be giving you more than the day I sold my little gold crosses, to obtain a little money for you. Oh, how your happiness made me ill then.

RAPHAEL: Your gold cross! Oh, wretch that I am! (with despair) Why are you so rich? Why aren't you vain? I can do nothing for you.

PAULINE: (passionately) Oh, your love, Raphael, your love, is worth the world! What! Your thought belongs to me. But I am the happiest of all!

RAPHAEL: Some one is going to hear us!

PAULINE: (with a little mutinous gesture) Eh! No one's around.

RAPHAEL: Well! Come. (offering her his hand)

PAULINE: (sitting on a stool at Raphael's feet) Hug me for all the sorrows you've given me. To wipe out the pain your joys caused me! For all the nights I spent painting my screens.

RAPHAEL: Your screens?

PAULINE: Since we are rich, my beloved, I can tell you everything. Poor child! Ah, how easy it is to deceive an intelligent man! And can you have white shirts, frills and the rest twice a week for three francs washing per month? Why, you drank twice as much milk as your money came to. I cheated you on everything.

RAPHAEL: (embracing her) Divine creature. But how'd you do it?

PAULINE: I worked until two in the morning, and I gave my mother my half of the price of my screens. And you, the other. (silence while the two look at each other, enraptured)

RAPHAEL: Oh—oh, one day, we will doubtless pay for this happiness with terrible sorrow.

PAULINE: (frightened) Oh, my God. Why do you say that?

RAPHAEL: You don't know. I have a talisman, you see—but, Bah! What's it matter to me! To live, without wanting you, without loving you. Rather die! Ah, indeed, yes,—the talisman. But I don't want to think about it any more.

PAULINE: (stupefied) Raphael! my Raphael, Come to. Your mind's wandering.

RAPHAEL: (making a violent effort over himself) You think so? Yes! It's joy, happiness. How beautiful you are, my Pauline.

PAULINE: (running her hand through his hair) And what about you! are you sweet! Isn't the Countess Foedora stupid not to love my Raphael? You don't know. When I saw you yesterday evening at that ball, I didn't say a word to you, and I escaped. I felt myself wanting to hang on your neck: in front of the whole world!

RAPHAEL: Are you happy to be able to speak? as for me, my heart is shaken. I would like to weep; I cannot. Don't pull your hand away. It seems to me, I could look at you like this for the rest of my life: happy, content.

PAULINE: Repeat after me. Say—my love!

RAPHAEL: We will never leave each other again, right? You will be my wife, my good genius. I begin to think a new life is coming. I am near you. I feel the air of happiness. (pressing her hand to his heart) Oh, be here. Always. Like this.

PAULINE: (tearing herself from his arms) Oh, my Raphael. I don't want anyone to ever come into this darling garret again.

RAPHAEL: We must wall up the door. Put bars on the windows and buy the house.

PAULINE: That's it. (picking up the papers on the table with a mocking air) And your manuscripts? Are you still thinking of them?

RAPHAEL: (laughing) Bah! I laugh at all the sciences.

PAULINE: (in a solemn tone) Ah, sir. And your glory?

RAPHAEL: You are my only glory.

PAULINE: (laughing) Were you unhappy, while scribbling all these little fly specs? You won't write any more, I hope.

RAPHAEL: No, never. (a discreet knock on the door, Pauline and Raphael jump apart)

PAULINE: Someone's knocking on the door!

RAPHAEL: (going to the door) Who's there?

WOMAN'S VOICE: Its me, Francine.

RAPHAEL: (stupefied) That voice! It's not an illusion?

VOICE: (impatiently) Open up, will you, Hamilcar.

RAPHAEL: No, no. I am not mistaken, It's really her. Just Heaven. (Opens the door abruptly. Foedora enters, dressed as a grisette of the Latin Quarter.)

RAPHAEL: Foedora.

FOEDORA: Raphael. (she wants to leave, but Raphael

gets between her and the door)

PAULINE: The Countess Foedora!

RAPHAEL: No, but Francine, the Grisette, Francine, the Courtesan. Oh, the clever woman who manages to accumulate the blessings of vice and the profits of virtue.

FOEDORA: (falling into a chair, head in her hands) Ah! I'm ruined.

RAPHAEL: Where are your valets, your cashmeres, your diamonds? A faded dress, a thin shawl. Fie, Madame Countess.

FOEDORA: (aside) Is this humiliating enough?

RAPHAEL: Are you sufficiently avenged, Pauline?

FOEDORA: (pulling herself together) Pauline! Ah, it's that Pauline, whose virtue you throw in my face like an insult! Ah, it's that chaste child, whose love, you said, purified your heart, despite its corruption! What's this white dove doing in this ignoble garret? By God, sir, I think you bold to dare to treat me as a courtesan before this girl.

RAPHAEL: (seizing her and forcing her to bow to Pauline) Wretch! on your knees, on your knees, before the Marquise de Villecraisnes!

PAULINE: Mercy! mercy for her, my Raphael!

RAPHAEL: Mercy for her! But you don't know everything, my Pauline! You don't know that this woman, as vindictive as cruel, as vile as degraded, conspired against my life.

PAULINE: Great God.

RAPHAEL: You don't know that yesterday, during the ball, hidden under a disguise she thought impenetrable, she enflamed a roughneck with jealousy, employing murderous slanders with her lover. Is it true, (to Foedora) Countess?

FOEDORA: (haughtily) And why deny it? You mortally offended me, Raphael! Did you think I was the woman to swallow your outrages? Reckless; whoever knows me, and doesn't fear to brave my hate. Yes, you spoke the truth! I swore your death; because, you living, my life is a disgrace and a torture! So, bad luck to you Raphael, bad luck to you. One failure has not yet worn out my vengeance.

PAULINE: (throwing her arms around Raphael's neck) Friend, this woman frightens me.

RAPHAEL: Calm down, my Pauline. I scorn her and do not fear her. (to Foedora) No, I don't fear you, Foedora! But I have better things to do than waste my time baffling your ambushes. With a single act of my will, I will annihilate your planned betrayals. Foedora, you hate me, right? Well, from this moment, I will that you love me. I will that you love me, madly, wretchedly, shamelessly, like I myself loved you. I will, that in your turn, you understand the tortures of a scorned love, trampled under my feet. I will it. I will it be so!

FOEDORA: (pressing her hand on her heart and struggling against a powerful feeling) No! That won't happen. I don't want it. Raphael, you've ruined me, you've tarnished me. I curse you—

RAPHAEL: You lie.

FOEDORA: Raphael. I ha—I love you, Raphael. (saying these words with an effort, as if brought to the ground by a superior power, she falls at Raphael's feet)

RAPHAEL: (pulling Pauline) Come, Pauline, come.

(Raphael and Pauline leave. Foedora remains on her knees, arms extended toward Raphael.)

CURTAIN

PEAU DE CHAGRIN, BY LOUIS JUDICIS

ACT V

SCENE VI

What You Find at the Bottom of a Pit

A picturesque view in the mountains of Auvergne. To the left, a cottage. To the right and back, usable rocks. Fougerol, Simonne, Father Jacques leave the cottage. Fougerol carries a hoe on his shoulders. Simonne is surrounded by several children. They speak the local Auvergnese dialect.

FOUGEROL: (embracing his wife) Come on. Bye wife! Now your soup has given me strength, I have to return to the mountain.

SIMONNE: Don't go get exhausted, like yesterday, when you caught a good dose of cold. We have to pay the

110

doctor and the apothecary, and Hell, shillings don't grow like weeds.

FATHER JACQUES: Shillings! That's all you dream of, Simonne.

FOUGEROL: Let her talk, father-in-law. She doesn't have a bad heart for all that. But, damn, you see, she holds the tail of the frying pan, (pointing to the children) and when you have to feed such a brood of brats—

FATHER JACQUES: Bah! I raised a dozen of them, I did, with the late Grandmother, and they never suffered, despite the good Lord's never sending pretty Parisians to our cabana.—Rolling in money.

SIMONNE: If the Parisian gives us some pieces of one hundred sous from time to time, I really earned them, that's what I think. It's clear you weren't the one who did the work.

FOUGEROL: Now that's enough of that. When you put yourself to squabbling, there's no end of it. Are you coming my way, father-in- law?

FATHER JACQUES: Hey, where are you going?

FOUGEROL: To the Val de Saut to dig out some ditches that the last rains have, for sure, hollowed out completely.

FATHER JACQUES: It's not very near. Still, I will go part way with you.

FOUGEROL: Bye wife. Bye, darlings! (hugging the children and leaving with Father Jacques)

SIMONNE: The old boy would really like to know what this gent from Paris pays me for his room: not dumb enough to mention that. He wants another new suit from the market at Clarmont... (looking off) My! My! A beautiful lady! What's she coming to do here?

FOEDORA: (trying to recognize the place, coming closer) My brave woman—Doesn't this cottage belong to a man named Pierre Fougerol?

SIMONNE: Pierre Fougerol? That's my husband, my brave lady, and I live here indeed, as you say.

FOEDORA: (aside) At last! (aloud) Don't you have a sick young man staying with you?

SIMONNE: Why do you ask me that?

FOEDORA: (giving her a purse) Apparently, I want to know.

SIMONNE: (pocketing the purse) That's a good reason, indeed. Well, yes, my beautiful lady, I have a young man from Paris with us. When I say young, you must know, he seems almost as ravaged as our grandfather.

FOEDORA: His name?

SIMONNE: His name? Ah, damn, he hasn't told it. My husband and I call him the Pale Face.

FOEDORA: How long has he been here?

SIMONNE: A week. Saving your respect, he came from Mont Dore as Doctor Rastignac tells me. A little gentleman, who's very nice, 'n' comes every morning for news of him.

FOEDORA: (aside) It is indeed him! My information was exact! (aloud) Where is he at, at this moment?

SIMONNE: To the right or the left. Every morning he goes to take his ease in a bit of sunshine. Not very far, my goodness. Ah, damn, he hasn't caught a fever doing it. I have the idea that today he went towards the lake. (pointing to the right) That way behind that row of trees. You'll find him stretched on the grass—like a rug.

FOEDORA: There my good woman. (starts to go to the right)

SIMONNE: It's time to make this brave gentleman's bed. It's not long after he rises, that he goes back to bed. What a pity! (calling the children) Come on. Hey, kids! Nicolas, are you going to come, scamp! (going back into the house with her children)

(Foedora stops at the back when she sees Rastignac and Pauline coming in from the left.)

FOEDORA: Pauline! Pauline here!

PAULINE: (to Rastignac) Raphael is in this house, right? (seeing Foedora) Ah! That woman again.

RASTIGNAC: Foedora!

FOEDORA: Yes, me! You didn't expect to meet me here, near Raphael, but if he refuses the attentions of his wife, it's necessary for someone to care for him, and that task belongs to me—because it's his love for me that's killing him.

PAULINE: What are you saying?

FOEDORA: I am saying that he loves me, Madame. I say that he still loves me! I say that his insults, his rage, proceed only from scorn and despair! I say that my love is all his life. And the proof is that you, who ought to make him so happy, cannot even keep him near you. That he's fleeing you, after a week of marriage, because he couldn't put up any longer with the horrible constraint it imposed on him. Poor innocent, you thought to triumph so with a first love? Undeceive yourself, Madame, Raphael still loves me. Raphael will always love me.

PAULINE: (to Rastignac) O my God! Could this woman be telling the truth?

FOEDORA: Doesn't he reject all your caresses? Isn't he dying of an illness that you are unaware of, but that I divine? Well, I came to save him. And I will save him.

PAULINE: You are forgetting, Madame, that Raphael is my husband, and that right belongs to me alone.

FOEDORA: And why didn't you exercise that right when he was near you? Why did you let him leave alone? As for me, with the strength of my cares and caresses, I would have restored his life to him. I saw him before his departure. His eyes had no luster, his hair had turned white. He's no more than an old man.

PAULINE: Oh, my God! my God!

FOEDORA: Here, now he's coming! Judge for yourself, the happiness you've brought him as your dowry. I am going to leave you with him! Let's see, Madame, if your love and care can recall him to life! Try, Madame, try. (she withdraws towards the back and observes)

RAPHAEL: (entering—holding out his arms to Pauline) Pauline!

PAULINE: Raphael! Ah, as for me, I was really sure of it: that you'd be happy to see me again.

RAPHAEL: Happy, yes. I wanted to see you, and—(with terror) O my God—that wish has been accomplished, that wish is tearing another shred from my existence. Ah, Pauline, it's you who are killing me.

PAULINE: What are you saying?

116

RAPHAEL: Oh—the talisman! The talisman!

RASTIGNAC: You promised me never to pronounce that word again, since, on my advice, you threw that supposed talisman into Simonne's well.

PAULINE: What! It's that peau de chagrin that Mr. Rastignac has told me of that's making you so ill? How crazy you are! Kiss me!

RAPHAEL: (pushing her away) Get out! Get out! Do you really want my death?

PAULINE: Raphael!

RAPHAEL: Get out! Get out!

PAULINE: He's driving me away, Mr. Rastignac, he's kicking me out!

FOEDORA: (aside, leaving) He doesn't love her. I was sure of it. (she leaves)

RASTIGNAC: (to Pauline) It's only a momentary distraction. Soon he will be more calm. Come! Come! (dragging her off)

RAPHAEL: (alone) What! I will tear myself away from happiness! I've left Pauline, my cherished wife! Pauline, who loves me. I'll have compromised all the beatings of my heart. I've fled from love, because each caress, each desire, robs me of a year of life. And nothing, no strength, no sacrifice, can withhold a step from Death which clasps me everywhere. To live without desires—a puerile and funereal chimera. Desire, why that's life, all life. Each glance is a desire. Each motion, a desire. In this moment, again, without willing it, without my intent—a misfortune! I desire to avoid this ray of sunshine. (after a silence) But also, Rastignac, could he be right? Am I only a poor maniac, and my imagination, struck by a conjunction of bizarre circumstances— Isn't my imagination the only cause of the illness that's killing me? Come on, I was crazy. Anyway, that talisman no longer exists, It's lost, annihilated. Ah, I feel myself reviving because of that idea. I breathe more easily and I want to—

SIMONNE: (running in) Sir, sir?

RAPHAEL: What's the matter?

SIMONNE: Look at this. Just now, pulling a bucket of water out of the well, I pulled up this funny marine plant. (she shows him the peau de chagrin, reduced in dimensions to a hundred sou note)

RAPHAEL: Great God.

SIMONNE: It must be used to the water, for it isn't damp or humid. It's like wood, and not thick at all. As the gentleman knows much more about these things than me, I thought this could interest him and please him. It's a curiosity and they say curiosities are worth money.

RAPHAEL: Yes, you are right. (giving her money) Here. This thing is very curious. Go, leave me alone.

SIMONNE: A crown! Ah, if I could find other like that in the well. I'm going to go back and see. (she leaves)

RAPHAEL: (absorbed) What! In a century of enlightenment we've learned that diamonds are crystals of carbon; an epoch where everything can be explained, where the police deliver a new Mahomet to the courts and submit his miracles to the Academy of Sciences— As for me, I am forced to believe in Talismans, in white magic, in the secrets of Albertus Magnus. (looking at the skin) That old Jew spoke the truth. Tomorrow, they will find me dead in my bed. (He remains motionless as if annihilated. Almost immediately, Job enters and goes to him.)

JOB: Ah, it's him! Ah, Mr. Rastignac had truly pointed him out.

RAPHAEL: (coming to himself) Who's there? What do they want with me? (recognizing Job) Job! Job! The Jew! Job! The Assassin! (getting up convulsively and seizing Job by the throat) Ah! wretch, I will be avenged on you before dying.

JOB: (getting loose) Release me, der Teufel. He's dying, that's certain.

RAPHAEL: (pursuing him) You're coming to see if I am dead, right? Rejoice, wretch.

JOB: Quite the contrary, my dear sir, I bring you health and life.

RAPHAEL: Health, life! Could you have that power?

JOB: Perhaps!

RAPHAEL: Speak then! Speak quickly. Don't you know that each minute that passes takes away a piece of my life?

JOB: (mysteriously) You haven't understood the Chaldean since you possessed the magic talisman?

RAPHAEL: No.

JOB: You did wrong.

RAPHAEL: (examining the talisman) What! Those mysterious lines engraved on the talisman contain my health?

JOB: Perhaps.

RAPHAEL: Always perhaps. But you yourself—didn't you tell me you were ignorant of this tongue?

JOB: That was my secret. A secret that needed your money, and you didn't have any.

RAPHAEL: What do you demand for this revelation?

JOB: Oh, almost nothing. You remember the pretty dancer, Euphrasie?

RAPHAEL: Euphrasie. Yes. And then?

JOB: Well, I did your will on that little demon. My millions, my poor millions eaten up, devoured, my dear Mr. Raphael. Eaten up. I am ruined, completely ruined, I sell padlocks on the boulevard.

RAPHAEL: I get it. That girl has abandoned you. Scorn her. Forget her.

JOB: Scorn her, that I do well enough. But forget her, never. I adore her, Mr. Raphael. I want to become her friend again.

RAPHAEL: What can I do about that?

JOB: With a word, you can restore my fortune. And my fortune belongs to Euphrasie.

RAPHAEL: Another wish. Why, it's my life you're demanding.

JOB: (examining the peau de chagrin) You still have two hours.

RAPHAEL: Two hours.

JOB: Less ten minutes. You aren't risking very much. In revenge, I am opening to you health, youth.

RAPHAEL: He's right! What do a few minutes more or less matter in measuring my agony? (aloud) I accept the bargain, Jew. But if you are deceiving me, wretch, bad luck to you. Whatever remains to me of a second existence after this test, I will employ it to punish you.

JOB: You wish that I become rich again?

RAPHAEL: I wish it; I will it. (Hardly has he pronounced these words than Job's wretched clothes are replaced by those of exquisite elegance. A rock opens and Euphrasie is revealed sleeping in the midst of a bed of roses.)

JOB: What's this! Mein Gott. Here I am, shining like the sun! (pulling a wallet from his pocket) A billfold! Full of bank notes. (noticing Euphrasie and running to her) Ah, the good girl. She returns with Mr. Green!

EUPHRASIE: (waking up and taking his arm) It's you, my little friend.

JOB: Yes, it's me, your little Job! (kissing her arms)

RAPHAEL: Now, the explanation of these lines?

JOB: Ah! Phooey! The Chaldean sentence—Listen,

young man (takes the skin and reads) "Let a mortal, man or woman, consent to give his life for your life, and I lose all my power." (returning the talisman to Raphael, in a sardonic voice) It's only a question of finding him.

RAPHAEL: Finding! Finding someone to consent to die in my place. Ah, that's a bad joke.

JOB: (pointing to father Jacques, who crosses the stage) Ask that old peasant. Good luck, Mr. Raphael. (leaves skipping with Euphrasie)

RAPHAEL: (dreamily, looking at Father Jacques) That old man. Like me he already has a foot in the grave.

FATHER JACQUES: (to Raphael) Oh, I can't do any more. Ah, my dear sir, where are my legs of fifteen! Wouldn't it be better to croak, than live, glued to the walls on one's house like a slug?

RAPHAEL: You no longer cling to life?

FATHER JACQUES: Such a life! I would give it away, almost, for two sous.

RAPHAEL: And, if someone offered you more?

FATHER JACQUES: (looking at him suspiciously) Hey, what is it that you're saying?

RAPHAEL: Didn't you say you are disgusted by life?

FATHER JACQUES: Me! Never said that! I never said that! Zounds! How you do go on!

RAPHAEL: At your age!

FATHER JACQUES: At my age! Don't say there's nothing left to do but put me in the ground. I am eighty-two years old. But, I really hope to live to be a hundred. Go on, go on. I'll still bury some. And much younger ones, you know. (aside) As for you—catch that. (sits on a stone bench)

RAPHAEL: Oh, how right the story teller was. All that we are, calls us to death. That's what helps us carry our burden. (noticing Fougerol, who enters from the left) Let's try this one. (aloud) Back already, Master Pierre?

FOUGEROL: Don't mention it to me, my dear sir. Such a beautiful garden patch, torn up, ravaged, broken into dust, not one spud remaining as large as a big toe. What a misfortune, my God. Exhaust yourself, break your back, to go naked and croak of starvation. Ah, mercy of

God! If I hadn't returned, I'd have broken my head a hundred times against the rocks.

RAPHAEL: And why did you return, Master Fougerol?

FOUGEROL: It's not for love of life, I really swear to you. A life for a galley slave, without pleasure or profit. But what do you want? I've got a wife and children.

RAPHAEL: And if someone assured the fate of your wife and your children?

FOUGEROL: (uneasily) Are you saying that to be funny?

RAPHAEL: If I offered you a million, in exchange for your life?

FOUGEROL: Ah! ah! That's very idiotic. You don't joke often, but when you set about it, you do it much better than others.

RAPHAEL: I'm not joking about that million, Master Fougerol. With a word, you can earn it. With a word, you can enrich all your family.

FOUGEROL: My opinion is that word must furiously

scorch your mouth.

RAPHAEL: Say only: I agree to die in your place.

FOUGEROL: Only that? That's not very worrisome. (aside) And that doesn't commit one to any big thing.

SIMONNE: (appearing in the cabin door) Fougerol! There you are, back already, malingerer. What are you doing there, planted on your legs like a lamp post?

FOUGEROL: I'm ruminating over something.

SIMONNE: You're ruminating about something. You have income at this time, so you can ruminate?

FOUGEROL: This gentleman over here proposes for me to die in his place. What do you say to that?

SIMONNE: What do I say? This is what I say to that. (to Raphael) You're a murderer, are you?

FOUGEROL: Offering me a million for that job.

SIMONNE: (changing her tone) A million? That's a fine thing.

FOUGEROL: (vexed) You think so, do you?

SIMONNE: A million!

FOUGEROL: Truly! So that's the effect it has on you? Much obliged! You'd wear mourning very gaily, from what I can see. (to Raphael) Your servant, Mr. City Slicker. Keep your millions! I'm not so dumb— sonofabitch! not so dumb!

RAPHAEL: I was sure of it. And, the refusal of the father made me foresee that of the son-in-law.

FOUGEROL: (to Father Jacques) What! Father-in-law. You refused such a fine opportunity to leave us some money.

FATHER JACQUES: Well, why didn't you seize it, since you find it so fine?

FOUGEROL: Oh, me! That's quite different.

SIMONNE: (weeping in a comic way) You! You're an egoist! You are not thinking of your poor wife, that you could make so rich and so happy.

FOUGEROL: You see that?

SIMONNE: Oh, these men! these men! (to Fougerol) Come on. Get to the orchard, and hurry to bring in your loose sheaves. Seems to me a rough storm is preparing. (they all leave, arguing)

(As Foedora enters, thunder begins to growl in the distance, and lightning illuminates the stage. The footlights lower bit by bit; by the end of the scene the stage is almost dark.)

RAPHAEL: It's only a question of finding someone, said the Jew. Easy thing, indeed! Must resign myself. A few instants still and the little life that remains to me. Fool! who would have been able to die, so happily, near Pauline. Near that angel that heaven sent you to soften the bitterness of your last hour!

FOEDORA: (entering, approaching him in a supplicating way) Raphael!

RAPHAEL: Foedora!

FOEDORA: Raphael. In the name of heaven, don't reject me! A word of pity, a word of pardon, my Raphael, I implore you. As I would implore God. (despairing) He isn't listening to me! What must I do, my God, for him to believe in my love?

RAPHAEL: I am going to die, Madame. From pity in your turn, don't trouble my last moments.

FOEDORA: Die! You're going to die! Oh, no, I misunderstood you. You didn't say that?

RAPHAEL: (looking at the talisman) Some minutes yet. If you love me, as you say, don't shorten them by forcing me—

FOEDORA: Die! why that's horrible.

RAPHAEL: I am condemned.

FOEDORA: But what to do? What to do to save him? Ah, if only I could give my life to save his.

RAPHAEL: (taking both her hands in his and looking her in the eyes with feverish anxiety) Are you speaking the truth, Foedora? Are you capable of such a sacrifice?

FOEDORA: (in tears) He doubts it! My God! Oh, bad luck to me.

(At this moment Pauline, accompanied by Rastignac, enters from the back. Seeing Foedora, she stops, struck with astonishment.)

PAULINE: (to Rastignac) That woman next to him! What's going on here?

RASTIGNAC: (stopping her) Listen. (they hang to the side, observing)

RAPHAEL: (with a wild joy) Foedora! If you believed that this devotion you are offering me could repurchase my life, if you were convinced that this substitution of one victim by another would be accepted by Death— would you still consent to it?

FOEDORA: Oh, my God! You frighten me and fill me with joy at the same time, my Raphael. I've seen you accomplish strange things which confound my reason. It seems to me you command a mysterious power—

RAPHAEL: It's here! but this power dominates me, in its turn. (pointing to the talisman) Masters both, slaves both. I accepted the contract.

FOEDORA: Ah, be blessed my God! Dead, to save him. Perhaps, he will shed a tear for me.

RAPHAEL: Then you consent to say these words, hand on your heart, this talisman in your hand. I desire it, I wish it, my death; life for him!

FOEDORA: (taking the talisman and placing it on her heart) Yes, I will say it! (raising her voice) I desire it, I wish it. (seeing Pauline, who approaches with Rastignac) Pauline! And I was going to sacrifice myself to unite them? How they would have laughed at me! Ah, ah, the two of you be cursed!

PAULINE: (snatching the talisman from her) It's I who will save him!

RAPHAEL: (placing his hand over her mouth) Pauline! I don't want that. I don't accept it.

PAULINE: (squirming loose) Death for me. Life for him!

(A clap of thunder followed by lightning. Pauline falls, motionless, on a bank of grass. Raphael rushes to her feet. Simonne, Fougerol, and Father Jacques rush out of the cabin and run, terrified. Foedora, motionless, observes everything.)

RAPHAEL: (kissing Pauline's hands with despair) Dead! dead! And it's I who killed her!

CURTAIN

EPILOGUE

SCENE VII

A curtain of clouds rises slowly from the stage and hides the preceding set from the spectators. It continues to rise, revealing Raphael's room laid out exactly as at the end of the first scene. Raphael is lying on his bed. Pauline, dressed as in the first scene, is kneeling next to him. Rastignac is leaning over the bed.

RAPHAEL: (dreaming) Help me, Pauline, help me. I love you, I—

PAULINE: Well, doctor?

RASTIGNAC: He's saved. This access of delirium is the last, no doubt. Look, he's waking up. Now, I can answer to you for him. He will live.

PAULINE: (on her knees) Oh thanks, my God!

RAPHAEL: (half rising) Pauline! Rastignac . . . what has happened to me?

PAULINE: You've been ill since yesterday evening, Mr. Raphael. But the doctor says you're going to be better, and I am really happy.

RASTIGNAC: Yes, I've cured you of a cerebral congestion! Ah! It's a fine cure. But, you are my first patient, and I have need of a testimonial.

RAPHAEL: A cerebral congestion. Then this contract, this peau de chagrin—

RASTIGNAC: Hallucination.

RAPHAEL: The Countess Foedora—

RASTIGNAC: A memory effaced by an extinguished love.

RAPHAEL: The inheritance?

RASTIGNAC: Ah! Thanks to God, that's the only reality

in the midst of the chimeras engendered by your delirium.

RAPHAEL: (looking at Pauline) The only one, you say?

RASTIGNAC: Yes, you are rich, my dear Raphael; not to millions, as you were saying in your dream, but honestly rich, so you can live independently. You are inheriting from your uncle Major O'Flaherty. Your family's notary came during your sleep to give us this news. You were in no condition to listen to him, but some words, doubtless, struck you, since this memory often came back in your delirium.

RAPHAEL: (looking at Pauline) Rich! I am rich and she loves me.

MADAME GAUDIN: (half opening the door) Well, how's he doing, this poor lad?

RASTIGNAC: Well, very well, Madame Gaudin. At last, you can make this poor child get the rest she's been deprived of since last night.

RAPHAEL: What! Pauline watched over me!

RASTIGNAC: With the devotion of a sister! Ah, she's an

angel, that little woman, and I don't know how you can ever repay her.

RAPHAEL: Well, as for me, I know. (taking Pauline by the hand) Madame Gaudin, will you grant me the hand of your daughter?

PAULINE: Heavens!

MADAME GAUDIN: (choked with joy) What are you saying? What, sir—

RASTIGNAC: Good, dammit. Your dream will, at least, have proved this: that true wisdom consists of not spending one's life running after happiness.

RAPHAEL: When it suffices to extend one's hand to grasp it. (holding Pauline)

CURTAIN

ABOUT THE AUTHOR

LOUIS JUDICIS was born on 24 November 1816 at Sainte-Brieuc, France. A well-known literary journalist, romancer, and playwright, he translated Boethius's Consolation of Philosophy from Latin into French, and also wrote a number of dramas, including vaudevilles. Among his best-known plays are *Peau de Chagrin* (1851; adapted from the novel of Honoré de Balzac); *Les Aventures de Mandrin* (1853; with Arnault); *Constantinople* (1854), and *La Veille de Marengo* (1859). He died on 24 August 1893 at Fontainebleau.

ABOUT THE TRANSLATOR

FRANK J. MORLOCK has written and translated many plays since retiring from the legal profession in 1992. His translations have also appeared on Project Gutenberg, the Alexandre Dumas Père web page, Literature in the Age of Napoléon, Infinite Artistries.com, and Munsey's (formerly Blackmask). In 2006 he received an award from the North American Jules Verne Society for his translations of Verne's plays. He lives and works in Maryland.

www.ingramcontent.com/pod-product-compliance
Lightning Source LLC
LaVergne TN
LVHW011204080426
835508LV00007B/600